FEARLESS FOOD

Allergy-Free Recipes for Kids

by KATRINA JORGENSEN

Capstone Young Readers
a capstone imprint

TABLE of CONTENTS

MAIN DISH

DESSERTS

WHAT IS A FOOD ALLERGY?

Our bodies are armed with immune systems. It's the immune system's job to fight infections, viruses, and invaders. Sometimes the immune system identifies a certain food as one of these invaders and attacks it. While our immune system fights, a chemical response is triggered and causes an allergic reaction. Reactions vary greatly from a mild skin irritation to having trouble breathing. Any time you feel you are having a reaction, tell an adult immediately.

The best way to avoid having an allergic reaction is to be aware of what you are eating. Be careful not to consume that allergen. If you are not sure if that allergen is in a food, ask an adult or read the ingredient label of the food container before eating. Unfortunately, allergens can sometimes be hard to identify in an ingredient list. Check out **http://www.foodallergy.org** for a full list of hidden food allergen terms.

Avoiding food allergens can be hard to manage, especially when they are found in so many of our favorite foods. This cookbook will take you on a culinary journey to explore many of the dishes you've had to avoid because of a food allergy.

Kitchen Safety

A safe kitchen is a fun kitchen! Always start your recipes with clean hands, surfaces, and tools. Wash your hands and any tools you may use in future steps of a recipe, especially when handling raw meat. Make sure you have an adult nearby to help you with any task you don't feel comfortable doing, such as cutting vegetables or carrying hot pans.

ALLERGY ALERTS AND TIPS

Have other food allergies? No problem.
Check out the list at the end of each recipe
for substitutions for other common allergens.
Look out for other cool tips and ideas too!

CONVERSIONS

1/4 teaspoon	1.25 grams or milliliters
1/2 teaspoon	2.5 g or mL
1 teaspoon	5 g or mL
1 tablespoon	15 g or mL
1/4 cup	57 g (dry) or 60 mL (liquid)
1/3 cup	75 g (dry) or 80 mL (liquid)
1/2 cup	114 g (dry) or 125 mL (liquid)
2/3 cup	150 g (dry) or 160 mL (liquid)
3/4 cup	170 g (dry) or 175 mL (liquid)
1 cup	227 g (dry) or 240 mL (liquid)
1 quart	950 mL

Fahrenheit (°F)	Celsius (°C)
325°	160°
350°	180°
375°	190°
400°	200°
425°	220°
450°	230°

BREAKFAST

HOMEMADE
TOASTER
PASTRIES

p.28

p.8

THE NO-EGG
SCRAMBLE

THE NO-EGG **SCRAMBLE**

WHEAT-FREE SOY-FREE NUT-FREE EGG-FREE DAIRY-FREE

Eggs are a staple in many breakfast foods. But you can create a unique take on a classic early morning meal by using protein-packed chickpeas. You'll want to scramble to make this delicious breakfast entrée!

Prep Time: 5 minutes

Cook Time: 10 minutes

Serves 1

Ingredients

⅓ cup chickpea flour

¼ cup water

¼ teaspoon salt

¼ teaspoon paprika

¼ teaspoon garlic powder

1 tablespoon olive oil

Tools

small bowl

measuring cups/spoons

whisk

non-stick skillet

spatula

Allergens Eradicated!

No major food allergens found here.

1. Combine the chickpea flour, water, salt, paprika, and garlic powder in a small bowl. Whisk ingredients until mixed well. Set aside.

2. Add the olive oil to the skillet and put over a burner set to medium heat.

3. Add the flour mixture to the skillet when the olive oil is hot. The oil will appear to ripple a bit when it is ready.

4. Allow to cook for about three minutes, or until the edges begin to bubble.

5. Use a spatula to break up the batter into bite-sized pieces. Continue to cook until the batter is cooked through, approximately another two to three minutes.

6. Remove from heat and serve immediately.

CHEF'S TIP

Include your favorite veggies or toppings such as mushrooms, spinach, peppers, or onions. Add them to the skillet after step 3.

BLUEBERRY BREAD

You don't need eggs to make fluffy, rich bread. Plump and juicy blueberries add a punch of flavor and antioxidants to this freshly baked loaf. Start your day with a sweet blueberry treat!

Prep Time: 15 minutes

Cook Time: 1 hour

Makes 1 loaf

Ingredients

cooking spray

2 cups all-purpose flour

1 teaspoon baking soda

1 teaspoon kosher salt

⅓ cup oil, such as olive oil

3 ripe bananas

¾ cup granulated sugar

1 teaspoon vanilla extract

1 cup thawed frozen blueberries

Tools

loaf pan

2 mixing bowls

measuring cups/spoons

wooden spoon

fork

toothpick

Allergen Alert!

If you need to avoid wheat, use a wheat-free flour blend instead of all-purpose flour.

1. Preheat oven to 325°F. Coat the loaf pan generously with the cooking spray and set aside.

2. Combine the flour, baking soda, and salt in a mixing bowl. Stir well and set aside.

3. Combine the oil, bananas, sugar, and vanilla extract in a second mixing bowl. Using a fork, mash the bananas and mix until they are mostly smooth.

4. Add the banana mixture into the flour mixture. Stir gently until the wet ingredients fully absorb the flour.

5. Pour in the blueberries and stir a few times.

6. Transfer the batter into the greased loaf pan. Then place the pan in the oven for about 45 to 50 minutes. The bread is done when a toothpick inserted into the center comes out clean.

7. Allow to cool for 10 to 15 minutes before slicing and serving. Store leftovers by covering completely for up to one week.

CHEF'S TIP

Transform your loaf into easy on-the-go snacks by making muffins! Instead of using a loaf pan, fill a muffin tin with paper liners. Scoop the batter into each cup, leaving about one-third of each cup empty at the top. Bake for 30 to 35 minutes.

APPLESAUCE **WAFFLES**

Crispy on the outside, fluffy on the inside, these waffles allow you to skip the eggs without compromising the delicious taste. Dive into the flavors of fall with these sweetly spiced waffles drizzled with maple syrup!

Prep Time: 10 minutes

Cook Time: 5 minutes

Serves 4

Ingredients

2 cups all-purpose flour

1 tablespoon baking powder

¼ teaspoon kosher salt

¼ cup granulated sugar

¼ teaspoon ground cinnamon

2 cups water

½ cup all-natural applesauce

¼ teaspoon maple extract

¼ cup oil, such as olive oil

cooking spray

maple syrup, for serving

Tools

2 mixing bowls

measuring cups/spoons

wooden spoon

waffle iron

fork

Allergen Alert!

Replace all-purpose flour with a wheat-free flour blend to avoid wheat.

1. Combine the flour, baking powder, salt, sugar, and cinnamon in a mixing bowl. Set aside.

2. Combine the water, applesauce, maple extract, and oil in a second mixing bowl. Stir until well blended.

3. Pour the wet ingredients into the bowl of dry ingredients and mix well.

4. Warm up the waffle iron and spray lightly with cooking spray.

5. Pour a portion of batter into the center of the iron (it should fill three-quarters of the iron) and close the lid. Follow the recommended cook time given by the waffle iron brand, or cook until golden brown.

6. Remove from waffle iron with a fork. Repeat steps 4 and 5 until all the batter is used.

7. Serve hot with maple syrup.

PEACHES 'N' CINNAMON OVERNIGHT OATMEAL

Oatmeal is one of many breakfast foods made with milk. Fortunately, almond milk is a great substitute that steers clear of dairy. Mix the ingredients and stow away in the refrigerator the night before for a grab-and-go breakfast you don't have to cook!

Prep Time: 10 minutes

Cook Time: 8 hours (inactive)

Serves 4

Ingredients

2 peaches

2 cups rolled oats

2 cups almond milk

½ teaspoon cinnamon

2 tablespoons pure maple syrup

Tools

cutting board

chef's knife

mixing bowl

measuring cups/spoons

mixing spoon

4 – 1 ½ cup food containers with lids

Allergen Alert!

If you are allergic to both
dairy and tree nuts, switch
the almond milk for rice milk.

1. Using the knife and cutting board, slice the peaches. Place the peaches in the mixing bowl.

2. Add oats, almond milk, cinnamon, and maple syrup to the bowl, and mix to combine.

3. Spoon the mixture evenly into the four containers and cover with lids.

4. Place in refrigerator overnight.

5. Enjoy for breakfast the next day!

CHEF'S TIP

Keep your cutting board from
moving by placing a damp paper towel
underneath it. This will keep your cutting
surface sturdy and stable!

BAKED FRENCH TOAST
WITH HOMEMADE BLUEBERRY SAUCE

You've probably heard that breakfast is the most important meal of the day. But what do you do when so many breakfast foods include dairy? Perfect for a weekend breakfast, this sweet, dairy-free treat served with a warm fruit topping will taste like dessert.

Prep Time: 8 hours 10 minutes
  (8 hours inactive)

Cook Time: 40 minutes

Serves 4

Ingredients

1 cup almond milk, plain

3 eggs

1 teaspoon vanilla extract

¼ teaspoon cinnamon

¼ teaspoon nutmeg

oil, such as vegetable oil

8 slices thick-sliced sandwich bread

Blueberry Sauce

1 cup blueberries

½ cup pure maple syrup

¼ cup lemon or orange juice

½ teaspoon arrowroot powder

Tools

large mixing bowl

measuring cups/spoons

whisk

8 x 8-inch (20 x 20-cm) baking dish

aluminum foil

small saucepan

Allergen Alert!

Swap rice milk for the almond milk if you need to avoid both dairy and tree nuts.

Trade plain sandwich bread for wheat-free bread if you're allergic to wheat.

Skip the eggs if you have an egg allergy. You won't miss them!

1. Add the almond milk, eggs, vanilla, cinnamon, and nutmeg to a large mixing bowl.

2. Whisk until the eggs and almond milk are mixed well. Set aside.

3. Grease the baking dish by rubbing some oil on the bottom and sides of the dish.

4. Tear the bread slices into 2-inch (5.1-cm) chunks and place in the baking dish.

5. Pour the egg/almond milk mixture over the top of the bread. It's OK if not all the bread is covered. When the bread sits in the refrigerator, it will soak up the mixture.

6. Cover the dish with aluminum foil and refrigerate overnight.

7. Preheat oven to 350°F to bake.

8. Leave aluminum foil on the dish and place in oven. Bake for 20 minutes. Remove foil carefully and bake an additional 20 minutes.

9. Make your sauce while the French toast bakes. Combine blueberries, maple syrup, and juice in a small saucepan.

10. Place mixture on burner over medium-high heat until it begins to bubble.

11. Turn the heat down to medium and add the arrowroot powder.

12. Allow sauce to simmer for about five minutes and then remove from burner.

13. Spoon out a portion of the French toast bake onto a plate and top with blueberry sauce. Enjoy!

PIZZA SCRAMBLE

Pizza for breakfast? With a few twists to the ingredient list, you can forego the milk and cheese. You'll want to set your alarm clock early for this spin on a classic that's easy to make and tasty to eat!

Prep Time: 10 minutes

Cook Time: 10 minutes

Serves 4

SOY-FREE

NUT-FREE

DAIRY-FREE

Ingredients

4 slices sandwich bread

2 eggs

1 tablespoon water

2 teaspoons oil

¼ cup pizza sauce or tomato sauce

4 tablespoons nutritional yeast

Tools

toaster

mixing bowl

whisk

non-stick skillet

spatula

large baking sheet

Allergen Alert!

Wheat-free bread can take the place of regular sandwich bread in this recipe.

Switch out scrambled eggs with chopped avocado or the No-Egg Scramble (page 8) if you have an egg allergy.

1. Preheat the oven broiler on high.

2. Toast the slices of bread in toaster until golden brown. Set aside.

3. Crack the eggs into a mixing bowl and add the water. Whisk until the yolks and whites are blended. Set aside.

4. Heat the oil over a burner on medium heat in a non-stick skillet.

5. Add the eggs. Stir with spatula until cooked and liquid is absorbed. Remove from heat.

6. Spread the pizza or tomato sauce on the toasted bread slices.

7. Arrange the scrambled eggs evenly on top of the sauce.

8. Sprinkle 1 tablespoon nutritional yeast over the eggs on each piece of toast.

9. Arrange toasts on a large baking sheet, and place in oven for about three minutes.

10. Remove from oven and serve hot.

CHEF'S TIP

Pump up your protein intake by adding some of your favorite allergen-free meat to your scramble!

BANANA-CHOCOLATE CRÈME
PANCAKES

Bananas + chocolate = YUM! Hazelnuts are an ingredient in chocolate crème, but you can get the same taste and texture with sunflower butter. Whip up a sweet pancake breakfast that your family will love!

Prep Time: 10 minutes

Cook Time: 10 minutes

Makes 8–10 pancakes

Ingredients

Chocolate Crème

½ cup sunflower butter

2 tablespoons cocoa powder

2 tablespoons honey

Banana Pancakes

3 bananas

1 ½ cups all-purpose flour

1 cup water

1 teaspoon baking powder

¼ teaspoon salt

cooking spray

Tools

2 mixing bowls

measuring cups/spoons

2 forks

chef's knife

cutting board

whisk

skillet

ladle

spatula

Allergen Alert!

Cocoa and chocolate are often manufactured with nuts. Check labels carefully, and call the manufacturer for details.

Replace the all-purpose flour with wheat-free flour mix if you're avoiding wheat!

1. In a mixing bowl, combine all crème ingredients. Mix well with a fork. Set aside.

2. Peel the bananas, and slice two of them into ½-inch (1.3-cm) rounds. Set aside. Mash the last banana well with a fork.

3. Scrape the mashed banana into a second mixing bowl. Add the flour, water, baking powder, and salt. Whisk until most lumps are gone.

4. Place the skillet on a burner set to medium heat.

5. When the pan is hot, add cooking spray to the surface. Then scoop ½ cup of batter onto the hot pan.

6. Allow to cook until bubbles appear around the edges.

7. Using the spatula, flip the pancake. Cook until golden brown.

8. Remove the pancake from the heat and place on a plate. Repeat steps 5 through 8 until all batter is gone.

9. To serve, spread 2 tablespoons of the chocolate crème on a pancake, followed by a few slices of banana.

10. Serve immediately. Leftover chocolate crème can be stored in the refrigerator for up to two weeks.

CHEF'S TIP

Don't want to monkey around with bananas? Slice up 1 cup (8 ounces) of strawberries instead for a sweet alternative!

APPLE **MUFFINS**

Grab the muffin tin and get ready to bake! These sweet treats are a perfect nut-free addition to the breakfast table. You'll fall in love with these fluffy muffins overflowing with flavor!

Prep Time: 15 minutes

Cook Time: 30 minutes

Makes 12 muffins

Ingredients

2 tablespoons flaxseed meal

¼ cup water

1 Granny Smith apple

2 cups all-purpose flour

½ cup sugar

1 ½ tablespoons pumpkin pie spice

1 teaspoon baking soda

1 teaspoon baking powder

1 ½ cups applesauce

½ cup sunflower oil

Tools

standard muffin tin

12 muffin liners

measuring cups/spoons

2 mixing bowls

whisk

peeler

cutting board

chef's knife

spoon

toothpick

Allergen Alert!

If you're avoiding wheat, make sure you use a wheat-free flour mix instead of all-purpose flour.

1. Preheat oven to 350°F. Line muffin tin with liners and set aside.

2. In a mixing bowl, combine the flaxseed meal and water. Stir with a whisk. Allow to sit for at least five minutes.

3. Peel and core the apple, and then cut into small cubes. Set aside.

4. In the unused mixing bowl, add the remaining dry ingredients. Stir to combine.

5. Add applesauce and sunflower oil to the flaxseed mix. Whisk to combine, then pour over the flour mixture.

6. Stir until most lumps are gone.

7. Drop in the apples. Stir until coated.

8. Fill each of the muffin cups two-thirds full.

9. Place in the oven for about 30 minutes. Insert a toothpick in the center of a muffin. If it comes out clean, the muffins are done. Remove muffins from the oven and allow to cool slightly before serving.

10. Store leftovers in an airtight container at room temperature for up to one week.

CHEF'S TIP

Want to add another flavor into the mix? Swap the applesauce for 1 ¾ cups pumpkin puree.

STRAWBERRY-AVOCADO POWER

SMOOTHIE

Looking for a quick-and-easy smoothie that's both healthy and nut-free? Like nuts, avocados are rich in B vitamins. Add in strawberries, and you have a delicious, nutritious drink.

Prep Time: 5 minutes

Makes 1 smoothie

Ingredients

½ avocado

½ cup frozen strawberries

1 frozen banana

½ cup milk

1 tablespoon honey

Tools

cutting board

chef's knife

spoon

measuring cups/spoons

blender

1. Carefully slice the avocado in half and remove the pit.

2. Scoop half of the avocado flesh into the blender, followed by the frozen strawberries, banana, milk, and honey.

3. Blend on high until smooth.

4. Pour into a serving glass, and serve immediately with a large straw.

CHEF'S TIP

Wishing for a thicker smoothie? Add a handful of crushed ice to your blender for a triple-thick delight!

Freezing your own fruit is fast and easy.

Strawberries: Wash and dry the strawberries well. Cut the stems off the tops of the strawberries, then slice each lengthwise.

Bananas: Peel the bananas and slice them into ½-inch (1.3-cm) rounds.

To freeze your fruits: Line a baking sheet with parchment paper and place strawberries and banana slices on it, flat sides down. Freeze for three hours and then transfer to a freezer-safe zip-top bag.

CHERRY PIE BREAKFAST
BARS

Pie for breakfast? It may sound like an early morning dessert, but these bars can give you a nutritious start to your day. The dates and cherries provide a sweet flavor without adding sugar.

Prep Time: 2 hours 15 minutes
    (2 hours inactive)

Makes 8 bars

Ingredients

½ cup pitted dates

2 tablespoons water

1 cup rolled oats

½ cup dried cherries

Tools

food processor

measuring cups/spoons

medium baking sheet

parchment paper

chef's knife

Allergen Alert!

Make sure you check the label of your rolled oats if you're allergic to wheat.

Many dried fruits and dates are manufactured with nuts. Be sure to check with the manufacturer to make sure they are safe for you.

1. Combine the dates and water in a food processor. Pulse until the mixture is mostly smooth.

2. Add the rolled oats. Then turn food processor on high for about 30 seconds.

3. Put the cherries in the food processor bowl and pulse about 10 times. The cherries should be chunky.

4. Line the baking sheet with parchment paper. Press the dough mixture into the pan with your hands, making sure it is spread out evenly.

5. Place in freezer for two hours to set.

6. Remove from freezer and allow to thaw slightly, about 15 minutes. Slice into eight bars.

7. Store leftovers in refrigerator in an airtight container for up to two weeks.

CHEF'S TIP

You can use any dried fruit in this recipe. Try apples, apricots, pineapple, or even mango instead!

HOMEMADE TOASTER
PASTRIES

You can have a fruit-filled blast by making toaster pastries from scratch, and you don't even need a toaster! Packaged breakfast foods at the grocery store might have soy, but these tasty pastries are soy free.

Prep Time: 30 minutes

Cook Time: 30 minutes

Makes 8 pastries

28

Ingredients

2 cups all-purpose flour, plus a little more for rolling out the dough

1 tablespoon sugar

½ teaspoon salt

⅔ cup shortening

¼ cup cold water

¼ cup your favorite jam

Icing

1 cup powdered sugar

2 tablespoons rice milk

1 teaspoon vanilla extract

Tools

large baking sheet

parchment paper

large mixing bowl

measuring cups/spoons

fork

rolling pin

pizza cutter

spatula

small mixing bowl

Allergen Alert!

If you need to avoid wheat, use wheat-free flour mix instead.

1. Preheat oven to 350°F. Line a baking sheet with parchment paper and set aside.

2. In a mixing bowl, combine the flour, sugar, and salt. Using a fork, mix in the shortening until it becomes crumbly, like wet sand.

3. Add water and mix gently with fingers until a dough ball forms. Add water if it's too dry.

4. Sprinkle a couple tablespoons of flour on a clean surface and place the dough ball on it. Use the rolling pin to flatten the ball into a rectangle about ⅛ inch (0.3 centimeter) thick.

5. Cut 16, 3 x 5-inch (7.6 x 12.7-cm) rectangles using the pizza cutter. Space evenly on the baking sheet about 1 inch (2.5 cm) apart.

6. Spread 1 tablespoon of jam on eight of the dough rectangles, leaving about ¼ inch (0.6 cm) of space from the edges.

7. Place the plain dough rectangles over the jam-filled rectangles. Press the tines of the fork around the edges to seal.

8. Using the fork, poke a few holes in the top of each pastry. Then place the baking sheet in the oven for about 20 minutes, or until the pastries are golden brown. Allow to cool for 10 minutes before icing.

9. Combine all icing ingredients in a mixing bowl. Stir well with a fork until smooth.

10. Ice the pastries by dipping a fork into the icing bowl and drizzling it over the pastries.

11. Store leftovers in the freezer for up to one month. To reheat, place in oven at 350°F for about five minutes.

APPLE PUFF
CEREAL

Start off your day with a bowl of apple cinnamon delight! These sweet puffs have a crunchy outside and a light, airy inside. Unlike many cereals from the grocery store, this recipe will keep soy away from the breakfast table.

Prep Time: 15 minutes

Cook Time: 15 minutes

Makes 2 cups cereal

Ingredients

1 cup flour

¼ teaspoon salt

1 teaspoon vanilla extract

½ teaspoon honey

½ teaspoon ground cinnamon

2 tablespoons applesauce

½ tablespoon olive oil

Tools

large baking sheet

parchment paper

food processor

measuring cups/spoons

spatula

Allergen Alert!

Swap out the all-purpose flour with wheat-free flour mix if you're avoiding wheat.

1. Preheat oven to 350°F. Line a baking sheet with parchment paper and set aside.

2. In a food processor set on high, combine all ingredients until a dough forms.

3. Remove the dough from the food processor with a spatula. Using clean hands, roll the dough into small balls, about the size of a grape.

4. Place the puffs about 1 inch (2.5 cm) apart on the baking sheet.

5. Put the baking sheet in the oven and bake for about seven minutes. Take out the baking sheet and swirl the pan around to roll the puffs over. Return pan to oven to finish baking for an additional eight minutes.

6. Remove from the oven and allow to cool completely before placing in an airtight container.

7. Serve with your favorite milk for breakfast or a snack!

CHEF'S TIP

Don't just eat this with milk for breakfast! Make a parfait with layers of creamy yogurt, fresh fruit, and crunchy apple puffs!

FLUFFY PANCAKES

Looking for a hearty breakfast that's quick, easy, and wheat-free? These pancakes stack up to their name — light, airy, and delicious! Ditch the wheat with this breakfast delight, and don't forget the maple syrup!

Prep Time: 5 minutes

Cook Time: 10 minutes

Serves 4

Ingredients

1 cup wheat-free flour blend

2 teaspoons baking powder

2 tablespoons sugar

pinch of salt

1 cup buttermilk

1 egg

2 tablespoons oil

1 teaspoon vanilla extract

cooking spray

maple syrup, for serving

Tools

measuring cups/spoons

large mixing bowl

electric hand mixer with whisk
    attachment

non-stick skillet

spatula

plate

Allergen Alert!

If you're avoiding dairy, you can make your
own dairy-free buttermilk! Simply mix
1 tablespoon lemon juice with 1 cup
dairy-free milk such as almond or rice milk.
Allow mixture to sit for five minutes and
then stir before adding to the recipe!

No eggs? No problem. Instead of
an egg, use one mashed-up banana.

1. Combine the flour, baking powder, sugar, salt, buttermilk, egg, oil, and vanilla extract in a large bowl.

2. Mix the ingredients until mostly smooth using an electric hand mixer set on medium.

3. Place the non-stick skillet on a burner set on medium heat and spray lightly with cooking spray.

4. Spoon about 1/3 of a cup onto the hot pan.

5. Flip the pancake over when bubbles start to form around the edges of the pancake.

6. Continue cooking an additional two minutes or until golden brown on both sides.

7. Place cooked pancake on a plate and set aside.

8. Repeat steps 4 through 6 until all batter is used up.

9. Serve hot with maple syrup.

PUMPKIN MORNING **MUFFINS**

WHEAT-FREE SOY-FREE NUT-FREE EGG-FREE DAIRY-FREE

Pumpkins may be a staple of Halloween, but with this recipe, you can enjoy them year-round! This festive fall sweet treat is packed with Vitamin A, an essential nutrient that keeps your vision sharp.

Prep Time: 15 minutes

Cook Time: 30 minutes

Makes 12 muffins

Ingredients

1 tart apple, such as Granny Smith

2 carrots

⅓ cup oil

1 15-ounce can pumpkin puree

¼ cup sugar

¼ cup brown sugar

1 teaspoon maple extract

2 cups wheat-free flour blend

2 teaspoons baking soda

1 teaspoon ground cinnamon

½ teaspoon ground ginger

¼ teaspoon ground cloves

¼ teaspoon salt

½ cup raisins

Tools

standard muffin tin with 12 cups

paper muffin liners

cutting board

vegetable peeler

chef's knife

spoon

box grater

large mixing bowl

measuring cups/spoons

Allergens Eradicated!

No major food allergens found here!

1. Preheat oven to 350°F. Place one liner in each of the cups of the muffin tin and set aside.

2. Peel the apple with the vegetable peeler. Then cut out the core by cutting the apple in half from top to bottom. Chop the apple into small cubes and set aside.

3. Peel the carrots with the vegetable peeler. Grate the carrots using the large-holed side of a box grater. Set aside.

4. In a large mixing bowl, combine the oil, pumpkin, sugar, brown sugar, and maple extract. Stir to combine.

5. Add the flour, baking soda, cinnamon, ginger, cloves, and salt. Stir until all the flour is absorbed. It's OK if the mix is a little lumpy.

6. Add the apples, carrots, and raisins to the bowl and mix.

7. Scoop the batter evenly into the muffin tin, filling each muffin about two-thirds full.

8. Bake for 30–35 minutes, or until a toothpick inserted into the center of a muffin comes out clean.

CHEF'S TIP

Freeze leftover muffins and grab one in the morning for a quick on-the-go breakfast!

MAPLE SAUSAGE BITES

Good (and delicious) things come in small packages! Store-bought sausages often use wheat as a filler, but these homemade bites are wheat-free. Spicy and sweet flavors combine in these tiny breakfast sausages.

Prep Time: 15 minutes

Cook Time: 10 minutes

Serves 4

Ingredients

1 pound (16 oz) ground pork or turkey

½ teaspoon dried sage

½ teaspoon Italian seasoning

¼ teaspoon allspice

½ teaspoon seasoning salt

¼ teaspoon ground black pepper

1 teaspoon fennel seeds

1 teaspoon pure maple syrup

Tools

mixing bowl

measuring spoons

fork

non-stick skillet

spatula

Allergens Eradicated!

No major food allergens found here!

1. Combine the ground pork or turkey, dried sage, Italian seasoning, allspice, seasoning salt, black pepper, fennel seeds, and maple syrup in a mixing bowl.

2. Mix with a fork until well-blended.

3. Split the mixture into 12 equal pieces and form into small, flat, round patties.

4. Place a non-stick skillet on a burner set to medium heat.

5. Add 3 or 4 patties to the pan and cook until browned on one side, two to three minutes.

6. Using the spatula, flip the patties. Cook an additional two to three minutes, or until no longer pink inside.

7. Repeat steps 5 and 6 until all the patties are cooked.

8. Serve hot as a side to your favorite breakfast!

CHEF'S TIP

If you are worried your hands will get too sticky handling the sausage mixture, rub a little oil on your palms beforehand!

RAISIN **GRANOLA**

It's important to eat breakfast before you start your day, but that can be tough when so many breakfast foods — especially cereal — contain wheat. With this recipe, you not only get a healthy substitute for cereal, you can take the leftovers with you for an on-the-go snack!

Prep Time: 10 minutes

Cook Time: 20 minutes

Serves 4

WHEAT-FREE SOY-FREE NUT-FREE EGG-FREE DAIRY-FREE

38

Ingredients

2 cups wheat-free rolled oats

½ cup wheat-free rice cereal

1 teaspoon ground cinnamon

¼ teaspoon salt

2 tablespoons brown sugar

⅓ cup pure maple syrup

⅓ cup oil, such as light olive oil

½ teaspoon vanilla

1 cup raisins

Tools

large baking sheet

parchment paper

mixing bowl

measuring cups/spoons

spatula

Allergens Eradicated!

No major food allergens found here!

1. Preheat oven to 325°F. Place a sheet of parchment paper on a large baking sheet and set aside.

2. Combine the rolled oats, rice cereal, ground cinnamon, salt, brown sugar, maple syrup, oil, vanilla, and raisins in a mixing bowl. Stir until the ingredients are coated well.

3. Spread the granola mixture on the baking sheet so it is mostly flat.

4. Bake in the oven for 20 minutes or until slightly golden brown.

5. Remove from the oven and allow to cool before serving.

6. Eat with your favorite yogurt, or splash some milk on top for a crunchy breakfast treat!

7. Store leftovers in an airtight container for up to two weeks.

CHEF'S TIP

Do raisins wrinkle your nose? Add any of your favorite dried fruits to this granola instead, such as blueberries, cherries, apricots, or bananas!

SNACKS

DAIRY-FREE   EGG-FREE   NUT-FREE   SOY-FREE   WHEAT-FREE

CHIPS AND DILL DIP

p.54

40

p.44

NO-CHEESE
VEGGIE DIP

LEATHERS

p.52

TROPICAL GREEK
YOGURT PARFAIT

Who needs eggs for protein! Jump-start your day with an energy-boosting breakfast. With layers of Greek yogurt and crunchy coconut, this parfait is a protein powerhouse!

Prep Time: 5 minutes

Makes 1 parfait

Ingredients

1 cup plain Greek yogurt

2 teaspoons pure honey

½ teaspoon vanilla extract

½ cup frozen diced mango, thawed

½ cup frozen diced pineapple, thawed

¼ cup toasted coconut flakes

Tools

mixing bowl

measuring cups/spoons

spoon

parfait glass or bowl, for serving

1. Combine the Greek yogurt, honey, and vanilla extract in a mixing bowl. Set aside.

2. Assemble your parfait by spreading one-third of the yogurt at the bottom of a parfait glass or bowl. Add one-third of the mango and pineapple. Repeat layers until finished.

3. Top with toasted coconut flakes and serve immediately.

Allergen Alert!

If you are allergic to dairy, use coconut milk or almond milk yogurt instead of the Greek yogurt.

Coconut is classified as a fruit. But if you have a tree nut allergy, please talk to your doctor before eating it.

NO-CHEESE
VEGGIE DIP

You'd never guess this cheese sauce doesn't actually have cheese. Ooey-gooey and so delicious — it makes all vegetables taste good!

Prep Time: 15 minutes

Makes 1 cup

Ingredients

2 tablespoons non-dairy buttery spread

1 tablespoon all-purpose flour

¾ cup rice milk

½ cup nutritional yeast

1 teaspoon mustard powder

1 teaspoon salt

½ teaspoon black pepper

Tools

measuring cups/spoons

medium skillet

whisk

Allergen Alert!

Make sure you use a wheat-free flour mixture if you have a wheat allergy.

1. Melt the buttery spread in a medium-sized skillet on a burner set to medium-high heat.

2. Add the flour and whisk until the mixture resembles wet sand.

3. Pour in the milk, whisking quickly at the same time.

4. When the mixture begins to bubble, turn the heat down to medium.

5. Add the nutritional yeast, mustard powder, salt, and pepper and whisk again to combine.

6. Allow the sauce to cook for about five minutes, or until it thickens slightly. If it is too runny, add flour 1 teaspoon at a time until it thickens to your desired thickness.

7. Remove from heat and serve hot to dip in with raw cut vegetables.

CHEF'S TIP

This dip can also be drizzled on top of your favorite cooked veggies. You can even stir in a few tablespoons with cooked pasta for another favorite — mac and cheese!

APPLE **SANDWICH**

Make your own sandwich — without bread or peanut butter! Cast aside the bread and use apples instead. Sunflower butter takes over the role of peanut butter so you can be nut-free without sacrificing the flavor.

Prep Time: 5 minutes

Makes 2 apple sandwiches

Ingredients

1 apple — your favorite kind

1 lemon

4 tablespoons sunflower butter

2 tablespoons of your choice of topping: rolled oats, raisins, pumpkin seeds, sesame seeds, or jam

Tools

cutting board

chef's knife

small round cookie cutter

measuring spoons

butter knife

1. Carefully cut the top and bottom off the apple, about ½-inch (1.3-cm) thick. Enjoy those pieces later!

2. Cut the remaining apple into four even slices for making two sandwiches. Set aside.

3. Using the round cookie cutter, cut the cores out of each slice and discard.

4. Cut the lemon in half. Gently squeeze a few drops of juice on both sides of the apple slices.

5. Spread 2 tablespoons of sunflower butter on two of the apple slices.

6. Sprinkle or spread your choice of topping over the sunflower butter.

7. Place the plain apple slices over the sunflower butter slices to make a sandwich.

8. Eat immediately, or store in an airtight container for up to one day.

CHEF'S TIP

Why put lemon on your apples? When you slice an apple, you expose the pulp to oxygen that causes it to turn brown. It's OK to eat apple slices that have turned brown (within a day or two of slicing). The acid in lemon juice forms a protective barrier that keeps your apples looking perfectly fresh!

BBQ ROASTED
CHICKPEAS

Combine a smoky BBQ flavor with the crunch of roasted chickpeas and you get a tasty, southern-inspired snack! These chickpeas are not only delicious but they are also a healthy treat loaded with protein.

Prep Time: 40 minutes
(30 minutes inactive)

Cook Time: 45 minutes

Makes 4 cups

Ingredients

2 15-ounce cans chickpeas
(also known as garbanzo beans)

2 teaspoons brown sugar

2 teaspoons salt

2 teaspoons garlic powder

½ teaspoon ground white pepper

1 teaspoon dry mustard

½ teaspoon cayenne pepper

½ teaspoon cumin

2 teaspoons smoked paprika

2 tablespoons olive oil

Tools

baking sheet

parchment paper

can opener

colander

paper towels

mixing bowl

measuring spoons

spatula

Allergens Eradicated!

No major food allergens found here!

1. Preheat oven to 400°F. Line a baking sheet with parchment paper and set aside.

2. Open the cans of chickpeas and empty them into the colander.

3. Keeping the chickpeas in the colander, rinse with cool water.

4. Line a clean surface with paper towels and spread the chickpeas on top.

5. Allow to sit for about 30 minutes to dry almost completely.

6. While the chickpeas dry, make your flavoring. Combine remaining ingredients in a mixing bowl. Stir until smooth.

7. When the chickpeas are mostly dry, transfer them to the mixing bowl. Stir to coat evenly.

8. Spread the chickpeas evenly on the baking sheet.

9. Bake in the oven for about 45 minutes, or until golden brown and hardened.

10. Remove from oven and allow to cool slightly before serving.

11. Store leftovers in an airtight container for up to three days.

CHEESY POPCORN

WHEAT-FREE

SOY-FREE

NUT-FREE

EGG-FREE

Ready to pop up a snack for movie night? You can impress guests with this cheesy, soy-free popcorn!

Prep Time: 5 minutes

Cook Time: 30 minutes

Makes about 10 cups

Ingredients

¼ cup popping corn

3 tablespoons olive oil

½ cup finely grated Parmesan cheese

Tools

large pot with lid

measuring cups/spoons

roasting pan

spoon

1. Preheat oven to 250°F.

2. In a large pot, place the popping corn and 1 tablespoon olive oil. Cover with a lid and set the burner to medium.

3. Wait until the corn begins popping, and then remove from heat after a minute to avoid burning. Wait until you no longer hear popping, then remove the lid.

4. Pour the popcorn into the roasting pan. Drizzle with olive oil and Parmesan cheese. Stir with a spoon to make sure everything is coated.

5. Bake in the oven for 20 minutes, stirring after 10 minutes. The popcorn should be crispy and coated with cheese.

CHEF'S TIP

Store leftovers in small zip-top bags for tasty snacks to grab on the go.

FRUIT LEATHERS

Reading the ingredient list of processed food can be overwhelming. There are dozens of ingredients, and most of them are too difficult to even pronounce! With only two ingredients, these fruit leathers are nutritious, delicious, and soy-free!

Prep Time: 5 minutes

Cook Time: 6 hours

Makes 24 servings

Ingredients

3 cups your favorite fruit

2 teaspoons honey

Tools

large baking sheet

parchment paper

measuring cups/spoons

blender

spatula

pizza cutter

Allergens Eradicated!

No major food allergens found here!

1. Preheat oven to 150°F. Line a baking sheet with parchment paper and set aside.

2. If your fruit contains pits, stones, or stems, remove them. Add fruit and honey to the blender. Blend on high until smooth.

3. Spread the blended mix evenly on the lined baking sheet and place in the oven.

4. Bake for six hours, or until the mixture no longer feels wet.

5. Remove from oven and let cool. Carefully peel the fruit leather away from the parchment paper. Use the pizza cutter to cut the fruit leather into strips. Place the strips on parchment paper or roll them up as they are.

6. Place in an airtight container for up to two weeks.

CHEF'S TIP

Need some fruit ideas? Strawberries, blueberries, peaches, pineapple, raspberries, grapes, or bananas work great in this recipe!

CHIPS AND DILL DIP

Skip the soy and make your own crispy, crunchy chips in the oven. Sink your chips into a smooth and creamy dip with a dill-flavored kick.

Prep Time: 10 minutes

Cook Time: 20 minutes

Serves 4

Ingredients

Chips

1 large Russet potato

3 tablespoons olive oil

1 teaspoon salt

Dill Dip

4 stems fresh dill

1 avocado

¼ cup coconut cream

2 tablespoons lemon juice

1 teaspoon dehydrated onion

½ teaspoon salt

Tools

large baking sheet

parchment paper

cutting board

chef's knife

pastry brush

spatula

paper towels

mixing bowl

fork

Allergen Alert!

Coconut is classified as a fruit. But if you have a tree nut allergy, please talk to your doctor before eating it.

1. Preheat oven to 400°F. Line a baking sheet with parchment paper and set aside.

2. Carefully slice the potatoes about ⅛-inch (0.3-cm) thick or as thinly as you can.

3. Evenly space them on the baking sheet. Make sure the pieces do not touch each other.

4. Brush both sides of each slice with olive oil. Then sprinkle with salt.

5. Place in oven and bake for 20 minutes or until golden brown.

6. Transfer chips to paper towels to absorb extra oil. Allow to cool before serving.

7. For the dip, pull the leaves off of the dill and chop into small pieces. Add to a mixing bowl.

8. Remove the skin and pit of the avocado and scoop the pulp into the mixing bowl. Mash with a fork.

9. Add the coconut cream, lemon juice, dehydrated onion, and salt to the bowl. Stir until smooth.

10. Serve immediately with chips.

11. Store leftovers in an airtight container in the refrigerator for up to three days.

SIDES

BAKED
French
FRIES

p.78

56

BLTA p.80

PASTA SALAD

THAI CHICKEN **SALAD** p.70

SPINACH-APPLE **SALAD**

Spinach is a great source of iron. You can create a nutritious and hearty salad with spinach. Get pumped up for this super salad topped with crisp apples and a sweet and tangy dressing!

Prep Time: 15 minutes

Serves 4

WHEAT-FREE

SOY-FREE

NUT-FREE

EGG-FREE

DAIRY-FREE

58

Ingredients

Dressing

¼ cup apple cider vinegar

½ cup extra-virgin olive oil

¼ cup apple juice

2 tablespoons pure maple syrup

1 tablespoon Dijon mustard

¼ teaspoon salt

¼ teaspoon ground black pepper

Salad

2 Granny Smith apples

1 cup dried cranberries

¼ cup sunflower seeds

4 cups fresh spinach leaves

Tools

glass jar with lid

measuring cups/spoons

cutting board

chef's knife

mixing bowl

tongs

1. In a glass jar, combine the cider vinegar, olive oil, apple juice, maple syrup, Dijon mustard, salt, and pepper.

2. Screw lid on tightly and shake hard for about 30 seconds or until mixed well. Set aside.

3. Dice the apples into ½-inch (1.3-cm) pieces and place in a mixing bowl with the cranberries, sunflower seeds, and spinach.

4. Pour three-quarters of the dressing over the salad and toss gently with tongs.

5. Serve on plates with additional dressing on the side.

Allergens Eradicated!

No major food allergens found here!

POTATO PANCAKES

Are you a "brinner" person? That's right, go ahead and have breakfast for dinner! Pancakes can be made with lots of different foods, including potatoes. Crispy on the outside, fluffy on the inside, these delicious egg-free cakes are great for any meal!

Prep Time: 10 minutes

Cook Time: 5–10 minutes

Serves 4

Ingredients

2 medium Russet potatoes

¼ cup olive oil, divided

2 teaspoons salt

1 teaspoon ground black pepper

Tools

vegetable brush

vegetable peeler

cutting board

box grater

medium skillet

4-inch (10-cm) round metal
 biscuit cutter

small juice glass

spatula

tongs

Allergens Eradicated!

No major food allergens found here!

1. Scrub the potatoes clean and remove the skin using a vegetable peeler.

2. Place a box grater on a cutting board. Carefully grate the potatoes using the side with large round holes. Divide the grated potatoes into four equal piles and set aside.

3. Place a medium skillet over a burner set to medium heat. Place the biscuit cutter on the skillet and pour 1 tablespoon of olive oil inside the cutter.

4. Stuff one of the piles of grated potato inside the cutter. Use the bottom of the juice glass to pack it tightly. Sprinkle with ½ teaspoon salt and ¼ teaspoon pepper.

5. Carefully pull the cutter up and off of the skillet, leaving the potatoes on the skillet. Use the tongs to pull off the cutter if it is too hot to touch.

6. Allow to cook about three to five minutes, then gently turn over to cook the other side.

7. Remove the potatoes from skillet and place on a plate. Cover with foil to keep hot.

8. Repeat steps 3 through 7 for the remaining potatoes.

9. Serve hot as a side dish at breakfast or dinner.

CHEF'S TIP

Top your taters with your favorite condiments: ketchup, salsa, or try applesauce and cinnamon for a sweet treat!

MAPLE-GLAZED **CARROTS**

You know carrots are good for you, right? But how can you make them pop with flavor? These carmelized carrots will treat your taste buds to a sweet and scrumptious surprise! They are the perfect side to many dishes.

Prep Time: 10 minutes

Cook Time: 20 minutes

Serves 4

Ingredients

1 pound (16 oz) carrots

2 tablespoons oil, such as olive oil

1 teaspoon salt

2 tablespoons pure maple syrup

Tools

baking sheet

parchment paper

vegetable peeler

cutting board

chef's knife

measuring spoons

Allergens Eradicated!

No major food allergens found here!

1. Preheat oven to 450°F. Line a baking sheet with parchment paper and set aside.

2. Peel the carrots with a vegetable peeler. Using a knife, cut the tops off each carrot. Then cut each carrot into 2-inch (5.1-cm) pieces.

3. Place carrots on baking sheet and drizzle with oil and salt.

4. Bake in oven for about 10 minutes or until carrots begin to brown.

5. Remove from oven and drizzle with maple syrup.

6. Increase oven temperature to 475°F. Bake an additional five to 10 minutes, or until the carrots have a deep brown color. Check after five minutes to avoid burning.

7. Serve immediately alongside your main course.

CHEF'S TIP

Sugar and spice make everything nice. Like a little spice? Sprinkle some cayenne pepper (about ¼ teaspoon) over the carrots during step 3.

CREAMY MASHED
POTATOES

Mashed potatoes get their smooth, creamy texture from butter and cream or milk. That's a lot of dairy products to avoid, but don't despair! Grab some spuds and get started on this alternate recipe that is even better than the original!

Prep Time: 10 minutes

Cook Time: 25 minutes

Serves 4

Ingredients

1 ½ pounds (24 oz) Yukon gold potatoes, plus water and salt for cooking

¼ cup chicken broth

¼ cup rice milk

3 tablespoons olive oil

½ teaspoon salt

½ teaspoon ground black pepper

Tools

vegetable peeler

cutting board

chef's knife

large pot

measuring cups/spoons

small saucepan

colander

potato masher

Allergen Alert!

If you follow a soy-free diet, check the ingredients list on the broth to make sure it is certified soy-free.

1. Clean potatoes under running water and peel using a vegetable peeler.

2. Cut into 2-inch (5.1-cm) cubes and place in a large pot.

3. Add enough water to cover the potatoes in the pot. Add 1 tablespoon salt.

4. Place pot on a burner set to medium-high and bring to a boil. Once boiling, turn the heat down to simmer. Cook for 20 minutes or until tender.

5. Place the chicken broth, rice milk, olive oil, salt, and pepper in a small saucepan. Cook over medium heat until it barely bubbles. Remove from heat and set aside.

6. Drain the potatoes and return them to the pot. Pour about half of the warm rice milk/broth mixture over the potatoes.

7. Use a potato masher to gently mash the potatoes. Add more liquid a little at a time until potatoes are fluffy.

8. Taste for seasoning. If they need a little more salt, add a pinch at a time.

9. Serve hot with Swedish Meatballs (page 96) or alongside any of your favorite dinner time main courses.

CHICKEN AND WILD RICE
SOUP

Craving a creamy comfort food?
Some soups use milk to create
a smooth, creamy texture. Coconut
milk takes the place of dairy in this
creamy concoction. Perfect on a cool
fall day, this chicken and wild rice
soup will warm you right up.

Prep Time: 10 minutes

Cook Time: 1 hour

Serves 4

Ingredients

1 onion

2 carrots

1 tablespoon oil

4 cups chicken broth

1 pound (16 oz) skinless, boneless chicken thighs

1 cup wild rice/brown rice mix

1 teaspoon dried thyme

1 cup coconut milk

salt and pepper

Tools

cutting board

chef's knife

vegetable peeler

large pot

measuring cups/spoons

Allergen Alert!

If you have a soy allergy, make sure your chicken broth is certified soy-free.

Carefully check the rice mix package for your allergens. Some brands may contain wheat or soy.

1. Peel and chop the onion.

2. Peel the carrots using a vegetable peeler, then slice each carrot.

3. Add the oil, onion, and carrots in a large pot over medium heat. Cook for about five minutes, or until the vegetables start to soften.

4. Add the chicken broth and bring to a simmer.

5. Cut the chicken thighs into 1-inch (2.5-cm) cubes while the broth is warming.

6. Add the chicken to the bubbling broth, and cook for 10 minutes.

7. Pour the rice mix and thyme into the pot and reduce the heat to medium-low. Cook for about 45 minutes, stirring occasionally.

8. Add the coconut milk and simmer for five minutes, until thickened.

9. Season the soup with salt and pepper a pinch at a time until seasoned to your liking.

10. Serve hot in bowls.

CHEF'S TIP

Cutting an onion can make your eyes tear up. To avoid irritating your peepers, pop the onion in the freezer for about 10 minutes before chopping.

SESAME GREEN
BEANS

Add some flair to the dinner table with Asian-inspired green beans. A play on green beans almondine, this dish replaces almonds with sesame seeds for a delicious crunch.

Prep Time: 5 minutes

Cook Time: 5 minutes

Serves 4

Ingredients

1 16-ounce microwavable bag
of fresh green beans

2 teaspoons olive oil

1 teaspoon toasted sesame oil

1 teaspoon coconut aminos

1 teaspoon honey

1 tablespoon sesame seeds

Tools

measuring spoons

skillet

tongs

wooden spoon

serving bowl

Allergen Alert!

Although sesame isn't considered one
of the top eight food allergens, it's a
very common allergy. You can leave
the sesame seeds off if you have
a sesame allergy.

1. Cook green beans in the microwave according to directions on package. Set aside to cool slightly before opening.

2. In a skillet, heat the olive oil over medium-high heat.

3. Carefully open the bag. Watch out for hot steam. Pour the green beans into the skillet.

4. Using tongs, toss the green beans around to coat with oil.

5. Add the sesame oil, coconut aminos, and honey.

6. Stir the green beans quickly as the sauce begins to slightly thicken.

7. Transfer the green beans to a serving bowl. Sprinkle with sesame seeds.

8. Toss gently with tongs to coat all of the beans. Serve hot.

CHEF'S TIP

You can use any green vegetable you like
for this recipe, such as broccoli, spinach,
peas, or asparagus!

WHEAT-FREE SOY-FREE NUT-FREE EGG-FREE DAIRY-FREE

How do you get a nutty flavor without the nuts? With sesame seeds! Peanuts are a staple ingredient in Thai food, but you won't miss them in this crunchy salad topped with a tangy dressing.

Prep Time: 20 minutes

Cook Time: 15 minutes

Serves 4

70

Ingredients

Dressing

¼ cup sunflower butter

2 teaspoons tahini
    (sesame seed paste)

2 tablespoons lime juice

3 tablespoons olive oil

1 tablespoon coconut aminos

3 tablespoons honey

1 tablespoon crushed garlic

1 tablespoon crushed ginger

½ teaspoon salt

¼ cup fresh cilantro

Salad

1 pound (16 oz) boneless,
    skinless chicken thighs

1 teaspoon salt

½ teaspoon pepper

2 tablespoons olive oil

1 bell pepper

1 cucumber

4 cups coleslaw mix

1 green onion

2 teaspoons sesame seeds

Tools

blender

measuring cups/spoons

cutting board

chef's knife

skillet

serving bowl

tongs

1. In a blender, combine all of the dressing ingredients. Blend on high until smooth.

2. Cut the chicken into bite-sized pieces. Sprinkle with salt and pepper.

3. Wash your hands, cutting board, and chef's knife after you have finished handling the chicken.

4. Heat the olive oil in a skillet over medium-high heat and add the chicken.

5. Cook the chicken on all sides, about eight to 10 minutes, or until no longer pink in the center. Set aside.

6. Cut the stem off the bell pepper, and then cut down the center. Carefully pull out the seeds and discard. Cut the pepper into small pieces and set aside.

7. Slice the cucumber into ¼-inch (0.6-cm) rounds and set aside.

8. To assemble the salad, place the coleslaw mix, bell pepper, cucumber, and chicken in a serving bowl.

9. Drizzle half of the dressing over the salad. Toss with tongs to coat all of the ingredients.

10. Add more dressing if necessary, then sprinkle with sesame seeds.

11. Serve immediately with leftover dressing on the side, if desired.

Allergen Alert!

Leave the sesame seed paste and the sesame seeds out of the recipe if you have a sesame allergy.

CHICKEN POT PIE SOUP

Indulge in all the flavors of chicken pot pie, but without the soy! Juicy chicken and tender vegetables combine to tantalize your taste buds in this creamy recipe. Warm up the burners for a hearty soup that will fill you up!

Prep Time: 15 minutes

Cook Time: 30 minutes

Serves 4

72

Ingredients

2 chicken breasts

1 tablespoon oil, such as olive oil

1 small onion

1 stalk celery

1 tablespoon butter

2 tablespoons all-purpose flour

4 cups chicken broth

1 cup milk

1 16-ounce package frozen vegetable mix

1 teaspoon salt

½ teaspoon ground black pepper

Tools

cutting board

chef's knife

measuring cups/spoons

skillet

tongs

large soup pot

spoon

Allergen Alert!

Milk and butter are a no-go if you're avoiding dairy, but no worries! Just use coconut or rice milk instead of regular milk. Soy-free, nondairy butter will work instead of butter.

If you cannot eat wheat, use rice flour instead of all-purpose flour.

Make sure you check the label of your chicken broth to be sure it is soy free!

1. Cut the chicken breasts into 1-inch (2.5-cm) cubes on the cutting board with the chef's knife.

2. Heat the oil in a skillet on a burner set on medium-high. Add the chicken and use the tongs to flip and stir. Cook about five minutes, or until no longer pink inside. Remove from heat and set aside.

3. Clean your knife and cutting board. Then chop the onion and celery into small pieces and set aside.

4. Add the butter to the large soup pot and melt over medium heat.

5. Put the onion and celery in the pot and stir gently. Allow to cook for about three to four minutes, or until the vegetables begin to soften.

6. Sprinkle the flour over the vegetables and stir until absorbed into the butter.

7. Pour in the chicken broth and milk, and stir quickly.

8. Increase the heat to medium-high until the soup begins to bubble softly. Reduce the heat to medium.

9. Add the frozen vegetables, salt, pepper, and the cooked chicken to the pot.

10. Cook for 30 minutes before serving.

ASIAN NOODLES

WHEAT-FREE

SOY-FREE

NUT-FREE

EGG-FREE

DAIRY-FREE

Looking for a quick and easy Eastern-inspired dish to complement your meal? Savory noodles and crunchy vegetables provide flavor without soy!

Prep Time: 15 minutes

Cook Time: 10 minutes

Serves 4

Ingredients

8 ounces rice noodles

2 cloves garlic

1 small onion

2 tablespoons oil, such as olive oil

1 10-ounce bag broccoli slaw

½ cup coconut aminos

1 teaspoon crushed ginger

1 teaspoon lime juice

2 teaspoons honey

Tools

pot

cutting board

chef's knife

skillet

measuring cups/spoons

spoon

Allergens Eradicated!

No major food allergens found here!

1. Cook the rice noodles according to package directions and set aside.

2. Chop the garlic and onion into small pieces and set aside.

3. Heat oil in a skillet over medium-high heat. Add the onion and garlic. Stir frequently to avoid burning. Cook for about two minutes, or until the onions start to soften.

4. Add the broccoli slaw, coconut aminos, ginger, lime juice, and honey. Stir well. The sauce should begin to thicken.

5. Cook for about three minutes before adding the cooked rice noodles.

6. Stir frequently to avoid sticking.

7. Serve immediately.

CHEF'S TIP

This recipe is a wonderful side for the Sesame Beef Skewers (page 103).

CHICKEN ZOODLE SOUP

When you're feeling under the weather, nothing beats a piping hot bowl of chicken noodle soup. However, most types of pasta are made with wheat. To avoid wheat, make the change from noodle to zucchini zoodle!

Prep Time: 20 minutes

Cook Time: 1 ½ hours

Serves 4

Ingredients

1 pound (16 oz) chicken
leg quarters

2 quarts water

2 carrots

2 stalks celery

1 small onion

1 tablespoon dried parsley

2 teaspoons salt

1 teaspoon black pepper

1 teaspoon garlic powder

1 teaspoon ground turmeric

½ teaspoon dried thyme

½ teaspoon dried oregano

1 large zucchini

Tools

large stockpot

measuring cups/spoons

vegetable peeler

cutting board

chef's knife

tongs

box grater

2 forks

Allergens Eradicated!

No major food allergens found here!

1. Place the chicken and water in a large stockpot. Set the pot on a burner set to medium-high heat until it begins to simmer. Reduce heat to medium and cook for about one hour until the meat is cooked.

2. Prepare the vegetables while the meat cooks. Peel the carrots with a vegetable peeler. Chop the carrots and celery into ¼-inch (0.6-cm) rounds. Cut the onion in half, peel, and then chop into small pieces. Set aside.

3. After the meat is cooked, carefully remove it from the pot using tongs. Place on a cutting board to cool.

4. Add the carrots, celery, onion, dried parsley, salt, pepper, garlic powder, turmeric, thyme, and oregano to the liquid and stir. Increase heat to bring to a low boil. Then reduce heat to medium and cook for about 30 minutes.

5. While the vegetables cook, grate the zucchini with the large-holed side of a box grater. Set aside.

6. Carefully pull the meat off of the bones (use two forks to avoid burning your fingers). Set aside.

7. Add both the zucchini and chicken back to the liquid. Stir for about one minute until the zucchini is cooked.

8. Serve hot in bowls with wheat-free crackers, if desired.

CHEF'S TIP

Craving carbs? Add 1 cup of rice to
the pot during step 4.

BAKED FRENCH FRIES

High in Vitamin C and potassium, potatoes are a great addition to your daily intake. Baking these delicious French fries is more heart-healthy too! Grab some spuds and create your own homemade fries with this quick and simple recipe.

Prep Time: 15 minutes

Cook Time: 30 minutes

Serves 4

Ingredients

4 medium potatoes

2 tablespoons oil, such as olive oil

½ teaspoon salt

¼ teaspoon pepper

Tools

large baking sheet

parchment paper

vegetable peeler

cutting board

chef's knife

paper towels

measuring spoons

mixing bowl

spatula

Allergens Eradicated!

No major food allergens found here!

1. Preheat oven to 425°F. Line the baking sheet with parchment paper. Set aside.

2. Peel the potatoes. Carefully cut each potato into three pieces lengthwise. Then cut each section into 4 or 5 pieces lengthwise, making long sticks.

3. Rinse the potato sticks and dry well with paper towels.

4. Place the sticks in the mixing bowl with the oil, salt, and pepper. Toss gently to coat evenly.

5. Spread the sticks on the baking sheet, making sure they are not stacked on top of each other.

6. Bake for about 15 minutes. Using a spatula, carefully flip over the fries. Bake an additional 15 minutes or until deep golden brown and crispy.

7. Remove from oven and allow to cool for five minutes before serving.

CHEF'S TIP

Get fancy with your fries
and add some fun flavors:
Italian Fries: Add 1 teaspoon
Italian seasoning during step 4.
Spicy Buffalo Fries: Add ¼ teaspoon
cayenne pepper during step 4.

BLTA **PASTA SALAD**

You don't need to make a sandwich to enjoy the classic flavors of a BLT. Bacon, lettuce, tomato, avocado, and pasta are the perfect players for a refreshing, scrumptious salad.

Prep Time: 3 hours 20 minutes
 (3 hours inactive)

Cook Time: 45 minutes

Serves 4

Ingredients

2 quarts water

2 teaspoons salt

1 cup wheat-free pasta

2 tablespoons Dijon mustard

2 tablespoons apple cider vinegar

¼ cup extra-virgin olive oil

2 teaspoons honey

3 slices wheat-free bacon

2 tomatoes

1 head romaine lettuce

1 avocado

Tools

medium pot

measuring cups/spoons

colander

medium bowl

small mixing bowl

whisk

skillet

cutting board

chef's knife

large mixing bowl

tongs

Allergens Eradicated!

No major food allergens found here!

1. Add water and salt to a pot and place on a burner set to high heat to boil. Add the pasta and cook according to package directions.

2. Drain the pasta and rinse with cool water.

3. Place pasta in a medium bowl. Cover and place in a refrigerator for at least three hours to cool completely.

4. While the pasta cools, make the dressing. In a small mixing bowl, combine the Dijon mustard, vinegar, olive oil, and honey. Whisk quickly until it is smooth and no longer separated. Add salt if needed.

5. Cook the bacon in a skillet until crisp. Chop the bacon on a cutting board. Set aside.

6. Chop the tomato and lettuce. Set aside.

7. With an adult's help, cut the avocado open and remove the pit. Scoop out the pulp and chop it. Set aside.

8. To assemble, put the cooled pasta, dressing, bacon, tomato, lettuce, and avocado in a large mixing bowl. Toss gently with tongs.

9. Allow to rest about 15 minutes before serving. Store leftovers in a refrigerator for up to five days.

MAIN DISH

DAIRY-FREE   EGG-FREE   NUT-FREE   SOY-FREE   WHEAT-FREE

SESAME

BEEF
SKEWERS

p.102

CHICKEN CRANBERRY SALAD LETTUCE WRAPS

p.106

SWEDISH MEATBALLS

p.96

CHICKEN NUGGETS
AND AVOCADO DIP

Who doesn't love chicken nuggets? But eggs usually help make the crispy, crunchy nugget coating. Not this time! These crispy bite-sized chicken nuggets and the creamy avocado dip are sure to please your entire family.

Prep Time: 10 minutes

Cook Time: 15 minutes

Serves 4

Ingredients

1 pound (16 oz) boneless, skinless chicken breasts

1 teaspoon kosher salt

½ teaspoon ground black pepper

½ teaspoon garlic powder

½ teaspoon paprika

½ cup all-purpose flour

¼ cup oil, such as olive oil

Avocado Dip

1 avocado

1 lime

½ bunch cilantro

1 teaspoon salt

¼ teaspoon hot sauce

Tools

baking sheet

parchment paper

cutting board

chef's knife

measuring cups/spoons

bowl

blender

serving dish

Allergen Alert!

If you have a wheat allergy, replace the all-purpose flour with a wheat-free flour blend or coconut flour.

1. Preheat oven to 425°F. Line a baking sheet with parchment paper and set aside.

2. Carefully cut the chicken into 2-inch (5.1-cm) cubes.

3. Sprinkle the salt, pepper, garlic powder, and paprika over all sides of the chicken pieces.

4. In a bowl, roll the chicken in the flour until coated.

5. Place chicken on baking sheet, leaving 1 inch (2.5 cm) of space between each piece. Drizzle oil over the chicken.

6. Place the baking sheet in the oven for about 10 to 15 minutes or until chicken is golden on the outside and no longer pink on the inside.

7. While the chicken bakes, ask an adult to help you peel the avocado and remove its pit. Place the pulp in a blender.

8. Cut the lime in half and squeeze its juice into the blender.

9. Pull the tops of the cilantro from the stems and add to blender, along with the salt, pepper, and hot sauce.

10. Place the lid on the blender. Blend on high until smooth. If the mixture is too thick, add a tablespoon of water and blend again.

11. Pour the dip into a serving dish. Cover and place in refrigerator until served.

12. When the chicken is finished baking, allow to cool five minutes before serving with dipping sauce.

CORN DOG BITES
AND HONEY MUSTARD DIPPING SAUCE

There's no need to go to the fair to enjoy this summer favorite. Did you know you can make an egg-free corn coating for your hot dogs with flax and water? It's easy, and the result is a delicious and fun treat!

Prep Time: 20 minutes

Cook Time: 20 minutes

Serves 4

Ingredients

1 tablespoon ground flaxseed

3 tablespoons warm water

1 cup yellow cornmeal

1 cup all-purpose flour

2 teaspoons baking powder

1 teaspoon salt

⅓ cup pure honey

½ cup milk

¼ cup oil, such as olive oil

4 hot dogs

Honey Mustard Sauce

1 cup coarse ground mustard

½ cup pure honey

1 teaspoon salt

Tools

standard muffin tin

12 muffin liners

2 small bowls

measuring cups/spoons

spoon

large mixing bowl

cutting board

chef's knife

toothpick

1. Preheat oven to 400°F. Line a muffin tin with paper liners and set aside.

2. Combine the flax and warm water together in a small bowl. Stir with a spoon to combine and then let sit for a few minutes.

3. In a large mixing bowl, combine the cornmeal, flour, baking powder, and salt. Mix well.

4. Add the flax mixture, honey, milk, and oil. Stir until combined.

5. Scoop the batter evenly into each muffin cup.

6. Cut each hot dog into three 2-inch (5.1-cm) sections and press a piece into each muffin cup.

7. Bake for about 20 minutes or until a toothpick comes out clean when inserted into the muffin.

8. Make the mustard dipping sauce while the muffins bake. Combine the mustard, honey, and salt in a small bowl and stir until mixed.

9. When the muffins are done, allow to cool for about five minutes before serving with the mustard dipping sauce on the side.

Allergen Alert!

Coconut flour or almond flour can replace the all-purpose flour to avoid wheat.

Be sure to read labels carefully on your hot dog packages. Soy, dairy, or wheat can be hidden in the ingredients list.

Soy milk or almond milk can be used to replace milk.

MINI MEATLOAVES

Meatloaf is a classic comfort food that is simple to make and yummy to eat. Applesauce makes these mini meatloaves fluffy, light, and absolutely delicious. You won't miss the eggs in this recipe!

Prep Time: 20 minutes

Cook Time: 30 minutes

Serves 4

Ingredients

1 small onion

1 ½ pounds (24 oz) lean ground beef or turkey

½ cup natural applesauce

1 tablespoon tomato paste

½ cup wheat-free bread crumbs

1 teaspoon dried ground thyme

1 teaspoon salt

½ teaspoon ground black pepper

Sauce

½ cup ketchup

¼ cup yellow mustard

¼ cup packed dark brown sugar

Tools

baking sheet

parchment paper

cutting board

chef's knife

box grater

2 large bowls

measuring cups/spoons

scraper

Allergens Eradicated!

No major food allergens found here!

1. Preheat oven to 375°F. Line a baking sheet with parchment paper. Set aside.

2. Carefully cut the onion in half, and then peel off the skin.

3. Place the box grater on the cutting board. Using the side of the grater with the large holes, gently grate the onion.

4. In a large bowl, combine the beef or turkey, applesauce, tomato paste, bread crumbs, thyme, salt, pepper, and grated onion.

5. Using clean hands, mix the meat until all of the ingredients are evenly combined.

6. Divide the meat into four equal pieces and form into loaf shapes on the baking sheet. Leave at least 2 inches (5.1 cm) of space between each mini loaf.

7. Place the ketchup, mustard, and brown sugar in a mixing bowl. Stir to combine.

8. Spread the sauce topping evenly over each loaf using a scraper. Then place the loaves in the oven.

9. Bake for about 30 minutes or until no longer pink inside.

10. Remove from the oven and allow to cool for five minutes before serving hot.

Did you know that fried chicken is often made with buttermilk? Acids in the buttermilk break down the chicken to make it juicy and tender. But don't take chicken strips off the menu yet! The acids in yogurt work the same way. Crispy on the outside, juicy on the inside, these chicken strips with dipping sauce are sure to please.

Prep Time: 20 minutes

Cook Time: 20 minutes

Serves 4

Ingredients

2 cups coconut milk yogurt

1 tablespoon dried parsley

2 teaspoons dried dill

1 teaspoon garlic powder

1 teaspoon onion powder

1 teaspoon lemon juice

½ teaspoon salt

½ teaspoon ground black pepper

2 boneless, skinless chicken breasts

salt and pepper

2 cups crispy corn hexagon cereal

¼ cup olive oil

Tools

measuring cups/spoons

mixing bowls

non-wooden spoon

plastic wrap

cutting board

chef's knife

gallon-size zip-top bag

rolling pin

plate

large skillet

spatula or tongs

Allergen Alert!

If you are allergic to wheat, make sure your corn cereal is certified wheat-free.

1. Combine the coconut milk yogurt, parsley, dill, garlic powder, onion powder, lemon juice, salt, and pepper in a mixing bowl. Stir well with a spoon and set aside.

2. Cut each of the chicken breasts into 4 equal strips (8 total), and sprinkle lightly with salt and pepper on both sides.

3. Separate 1 cup of the yogurt mix and place in a second mixing bowl.

4. Add chicken to one of the bowls and stir to coat.

5. Cover the other bowl of yogurt mix with plastic wrap and place in refrigerator until later.

6. Pour the corn cereal into the zip-top bag and seal. Set the bag on a counter or surface. Gently crush the cereal by tapping the bag with the rolling pin, until the cereal resembles breadcrumbs. Pour the crushed cereal onto a plate.

7. Set a large skillet on a burner on medium heat. Add the oil.

8. Roll each piece of chicken around in the crumbs, until covered.

9. Place the chicken in the skillet, avoiding splatters. Cook for about five minutes per side or until golden brown on the outside and no longer pink inside.

10. Remove chicken from skillet and place on a plate lined with paper towels to soak up excess oil.

11. Serve hot with remaining yogurt dipping sauce.

TACO SALAD

Head south of the border for this dairy-free delight! Crispy and fresh, this Mexican-inspired salad avoids the cheese and sour cream but adds many tantalizing ingredients.

Prep Time: 45 minutes (30 minutes inactive)

Cook Time: 20 minutes

Serves 4

Ingredients

2 boneless, skinless chicken breasts

2 tablespoons olive oil

1 tablespoon lime juice

1 tablespoon ground cumin

2 tablespoons chili powder

1 teaspoon dried oregano

½ teaspoon salt

½ teaspoon ground black pepper

1 10-ounce bag chopped romaine lettuce

2 ripe tomatoes

1 small red onion, peeled

1 10-ounce can corn, drained

1 cup corn tortilla strips

Avocado Dressing

2 ripe avocados

1 8-ounce can full-fat coconut milk

2 tablespoons lime juice

1 teaspoon dried dill

1 teaspoon garlic powder

1 teaspoon dried thyme

½ teaspoon salt

½ teaspoon ground black pepper

Tools

2 cutting boards, one for raw chicken and one for vegetables

chef's knife

2 large mixing bowls

measuring spoons

whisk

plastic wrap

blender

large skillet

tongs

1. Cut the pieces of chicken into 1-inch (2.5-cm) chunks and set aside.

2. Whisk together the oil, lime juice, cumin, chili powder, oregano, salt, and pepper in one large mixing bowl until blended.

3. Add the chicken, and stir to coat. Cover with plastic wrap and allow chicken to marinate for 30 minutes.

4. Make the avocado cream dressing while the chicken marinates. Ask an adult to help you cut the avocados in half and remove the pits. Scoop out the pulp and place in a blender with remaining dressing ingredients.

5. Blend on high until consistency is thin, adding water 1 tablespoon at a time, if necessary.

6. Chop tomatoes and onion and set aside.

7. When the chicken is done marinating, heat a large skillet over a burner set to medium.

8. Add the chicken and marinade to the skillet. Stir occasionally while the meat cooks, about seven minutes, or until no longer pink.

9. Assemble the salad in the second large mixing bowl. Add the lettuce, tomatoes, onion, corn, and chicken. Drizzle the avocado dressing lightly over the salad and toss gently with tongs to mix. Top with the tortilla strips and serve with more avocado cream dressing, if desired.

Allergens Eradicated!

No major food allergens found here!

CREAMY PASTA CARBONARA

Traditionally, this dish is made
with both cream and eggs. But you
won't be missing them at all with
this flavorful pasta bowl.

Prep Time: 10 minutes

Cook Time: 20 minutes

Serves 4

Ingredients

4 slices thick-sliced bacon

1 small onion

1 tablespoons olive oil

8 ounces uncooked spaghetti pasta, plus water and salt for cooking

1 ½ cups plain rice milk

3 teaspoons arrowroot powder

1 teaspoon garlic powder

1 cup frozen peas

2 tablespoons nutritional yeast

salt and pepper

Tools

cutting board

chef's knife

large skillet

measuring cups/spoons

large pot

colander

whisk

tongs

Allergen Alert!

If you have a wheat allergy, be aware of your bacon! Make sure the label reads certified gluten-free.

You should also swap the semolina pasta with wheat-free pasta if you are allergic to wheat.

1. Carefully cut the bacon into ½-inch (1.3-cm) pieces using a cutting board and chef's knife. Place bacon pieces in a large skillet.

2. Peel and chop the onion and add to the skillet along with the olive oil.

3. Place skillet with bacon, onion, and olive oil onto a burner set to medium heat. Slowly cook until the bacon is crisp and onions tender. Look out for splatters! Remove from heat when done.

4. Ask an adult to help you drain the fat from the skillet, and set aside.

5. Fill a large pot ¾ full of water and add 1 tablespoon salt. Put the pot on a burner over high heat until it begins to boil.

6. Reduce the heat and add the pasta, cooking according to package directions until done. Drain and set aside.

7. Place the skillet with the bacon and onions back on a burner on medium-high heat.

8. Add rice milk, arrowroot powder, and garlic powder to the pan. Whisk quickly to dissolve powders.

9. When the liquid starts to bubble, reduce the heat to medium and continue whisking until it thickens. Add more arrowroot powder, 1 teaspoon at a time for more thickness.

10. Add the drained pasta, frozen peas, and nutritional yeast to the skillet and toss gently with tongs. Taste sauce, and add salt and pepper as needed, a pinch at a time.

11. Serve hot with extra nutritional yeast on the side to sprinkle on top.

SWEDISH MEATBALLS

One of Scandinavia's prized dishes gets its fame for soft and tender meatballs smothered in a cream sauce. You can re-create this savory entrée without the cream! This delicious, comforting dish tastes great on top of the Creamy Mashed Potatoes.

Prep Time: 30 minutes

Cook Time: 30 minutes

Serves 4

Ingredients

Meatballs

1 small onion

1 pound (16 oz) ground pork

1 teaspoon salt

½ teaspoon pepper

¼ teaspoon ground nutmeg

¼ teaspoon ground cardamom

Sauce

2 cups beef broth

½ cup coconut cream

2 tablespoons arrowroot powder

salt and pepper, to taste

Tools

large baking sheet

parchment paper

cutting board

chef's knife

box grater

large mixing bowl

measuring cups/spoons

large skillet

whisk

Allergen Alert!

If you follow a soy-free diet, check the ingredients list on the beef broth to make sure it is certified free of soy.

1. Preheat oven to 375°F. Line a large baking sheet with parchment paper and set aside.

2. Cut the onion in half and peel the skin off using the cutting board and chef's knife. Then grate it using the side of the box grater with the smallest holes.

3. Place grated onion in the large mixing bowl and set aside.

4. Add the pork, salt, pepper, nutmeg, and cardamom to the bowl.

5. Squish the mixture with your hands until everything is mixed well.

6. Use a spoon to roll meatballs. Evenly scoop out portions (about 2 tablespoons each) of the meat mixture, and roll between palms.

7. Place the meatballs on the baking sheet ½ inch (1.3 cm) apart. Bake in the oven for about 20 minutes or until no longer pink inside.

8. Make the sauce while the meatballs bake. Combine the beef broth, coconut cream, and arrowroot powder in a large skillet. Whisk ingredients quickly to dissolve.

9. Bring mixture to a low simmer over medium heat until thickened slightly.

10. Add the meatballs to the skillet with the sauce when they are done and stir well. Add salt and pepper a pinch at a time until seasoned to your liking.

11. Serve hot. This dish also tastes great on top of the Creamy Mashed Potatoes (page 64). Add a little sauce to top it off.

PUMPKIN SEED PESTO
PASTA

You may get tongue-tied trying to say this recipe name, but you can reward your taste buds with this light and fresh pasta. Pesto is usually made with pine nuts, but pumpkin seeds allow you to keep nuts out of the recipe.

Prep Time: 5 minutes

Cook Time: 15 minutes

Serves 4

Ingredients

1 gallon water

2 tablespoons salt

8 ounces pasta, any shape

Pesto

2 cups fresh basil leaves

¼ cup extra virgin olive oil

¼ cup pumpkin seeds

2 garlic cloves

½ teaspoon lemon juice

¼ cup shredded Parmesan cheese

½ teaspoon salt

¼ teaspoon ground black pepper

Tools

large pot

measuring cups/spoons

blender

colander

serving bowl

tongs

1. Place water in a large pot with salt. Set pot on a burner set to high.

2. When the water begins to boil, add the pasta. Reduce heat to a low boil. Cook according to package directions.

3. Combine all pesto ingredients in a blender. Blend on high until smooth. Set aside.

4. When the pasta is cooked, carefully drain into a colander.

5. Transfer pasta to a serving bowl and add half of the pesto.

6. Toss gently with tongs until the pasta is coated. Add more pesto if desired.

7. Serve immediately. Store leftover pesto in an airtight container in a refrigerator for up to three days.

Allergen Alert!

Do you need to avoid dairy? Trade the Parmesan cheese for equal parts nutritional yeast.

Egg-free or wheat-free pasta can be used in place of regular pasta.

HONEY GARLIC
CHICKEN WINGS

Want something finger-lickin' good but also easy to make? These sticky and sweet glazed chicken wings are sure to please. Whether you're serving them for a jazzed-up weeknight meal or a tantalizing party appetizer, these crispy wings with bold flavor will be the star!

Prep Time: 15 minutes

Cook Time: 2 hours 40 minutes
   (2 ½ hours inactive)

Serves 4 as a meal, 8 as an appetizer

Ingredients

2 tablespoons crushed garlic

¼ cup olive oil

¼ cup honey

2 tablespoons soy sauce

2 tablespoons brown sugar

1 teaspoon cornstarch

2 pounds (32 oz) bone-in chicken wings
   (about 24 wings)

1 teaspoon salt

½ teaspoon black pepper

1 tablespoon sesame seeds

Tools

measuring cups/spoons

medium mixing bowl

whisk

cutting board

paper towels

tongs

2 quart slow cooker

large baking sheet

parchment paper

ladle

Allergen Alert!

If you're allergic to soy, you can
use an equal amount of coconut aminos
instead of soy sauce.

Leave the sesame seeds off
if you have a sesame allergy.

1. Combine the first six ingredients in a medium mixing bowl. Whisk until smooth. Set aside.

2. Place the chicken wings on a cutting board and pat dry with paper towels.

3. Sprinkle salt and pepper on both sides of the wings. Pat with hands to make sure it sticks. Wash your hands when done.

4. Use tongs to place the wings in the bottom of the slow cooker. Pour sauce over top. Stir to coat.

5. Put the lid on the slow cooker and set on high for two and a half hours.

6. When the wings are almost done, preheat oven to 450°F. Line a large baking sheet with parchment paper and set aside.

7. When the wings are done, use tongs to place them on the baking sheet about ½ inch (1.3 cm) apart.

8. Place in the oven for about 10 minutes, or until the skin is slightly crispy and browned.

9. Ladle the remaining sauce over the wings. Toss to coat.

10. Sprinkle with sesame seeds and serve hot.

CHEF'S TIP

You don't want to use chicken wings? You can make
this recipe with chicken thighs or drumsticks. Just
add an hour of cooking time to your slow cooker
(3 ½ hours, instead of 2 ½).

SESAME BEEF SKEWERS

WHEAT-FREE
SOY-FREE
NUT-FREE
EGG-FREE
DAIRY-FREE

Typical Asian cuisine uses soy as a key ingredient. But you can still enjoy a similar soy flavor with coconut aminos! Give your skewers a zingy Asian flare with this easy recipe.

Prep Time: 1 hour 15 minutes
(1 hour inactive)

Cook Time: 4 minutes

Makes 12 skewers

102

Ingredients

1 pound (16 oz) flank steak

2 cloves garlic

2 green onions

1-inch piece of fresh ginger

¼ cup coconut aminos

2 tablespoons chili-garlic sauce

2 tablespoons toasted sesame oil

1 tablespoon rice wine vinegar

cooking spray

Tools

cutting board

chef's knife

mixing bowl

micro-grater

measuring cups/spoons

whisk

gallon-size zip-top bag

12 wooden skewers

baking sheet

aluminum foil

Allergens Eradicated!

No major food allergens found here!

1. Using the cutting board and chef's knife, cut the flank steak into long, ½-inch (1.3-cm) thick strips. Set aside.

2. Clean your cutting board and knife. Then chop the garlic and green onions into very small pieces and set aside.

3. Using the micro-grater, carefully grate the ginger over a cutting board. Add it to the mixing bowl, along with the garlic and onions.

4. Add the coconut aminos, chili-garlic sauce, sesame oil, and vinegar to the mixing bowl. Whisk until mixed.

5. Place the marinade and beef into a zip-top bag. Using fingers, squish the beef until coated. Place the bag in the refrigerator for one hour.

6. Soak skewers in water while meat marinates.

7. Place the oven rack 4 to 6 inches (10 to 15 cm) below the broiler. Set the broiler on high. Line a baking sheet with aluminum foil. Place a wire cooling rack on top of the aluminum foil and spray with cooking spray.

8. Thread the skewers through the slices of meat. Discard the leftover marinade.

9. Place the skewers on the wire cooling rack. Then set the baking sheet in the oven.

10. Use tongs to turn over the skewers after two minutes. Cook an additional two minutes.

11. Remove from the oven and allow to cool for five minutes before serving hot.

GREEK TURKEY BURGERS
WITH CUCUMBER TZATZIKI

Forget the traditional burger!
Go Greek by adding a cool and
refreshing cucumber tzatziki sauce
to a traditional turkey burger.

Prep Time: 15 minutes

Cook Time: 15 minutes

Makes 4 burgers

Ingredients

Cucumber Tzatziki

½ English cucumber

1 clove garlic

¼ cup coconut cream

1 teaspoon lemon juice

¼ teaspoon salt

⅛ teaspoon ground black pepper

Turkey Burgers

2 cloves garlic

¼ cup fresh oregano

1 lemon

1 teaspoon salt

½ teaspoon ground black pepper

1 ½ pounds (24 oz) ground turkey

1 tablespoon olive oil

4 mini wheat-free hamburger buns

Tools

cutting board

chef's knife

grater

2 mixing bowls

measuring cups/spoons

micro-grater

skillet

spatula

Allergen Alert!

Read the slider bun label carefully to make sure it is certified soy-free.

1. For the tzatziki, cut the cucumber in half lengthwise. Then scoop out the seeds with a spoon. Grate half of the cucumber and place in a mixing bowl. Set aside the other half.

2. Chop the garlic finely and place in a mixing bowl. Add the coconut cream, lemon juice, salt, and pepper to the mixing bowl. Stir to combine and store in refrigerator until ready to use.

3. For the burgers, chop the garlic finely and toss in a mixing bowl.

4. Pull the leaves off of the fresh oregano and chop lightly. Add to bowl.

5. Zest the yellow part of the lemon peel using the micro-grater over the mixing bowl.

6. Add the salt, ground pepper, and ground turkey to the bowl. Mix gently with your hands until all ingredients are evenly mixed.

7. Divide the meat into 4 evenly-shaped balls. Flatten into round patties.

8. Heat the oil in the skillet over medium heat. Carefully place the patties in the hot oil, avoiding splatters.

9. Cook about six minutes on each side, or until no longer pink inside. Use the spatula for flipping.

10. To assemble the burgers, place 2 tablespoons of the tzatziki on top of the bottom half of each bun. Then set a burger on top of the tzatziki followed by the top half of the bun.

11. Serve immediately.

CHICKEN CRANBERRY SALAD
LETTUCE WRAPS

Crispy lettuce makes the perfect
package for delicious ingredients
in these tasty wraps! Mix in a tangy
homemade sauce to go with your
scrumptious meal.

Prep Time: 15 minutes

Cook Time: 5 minutes

Makes 4 wraps

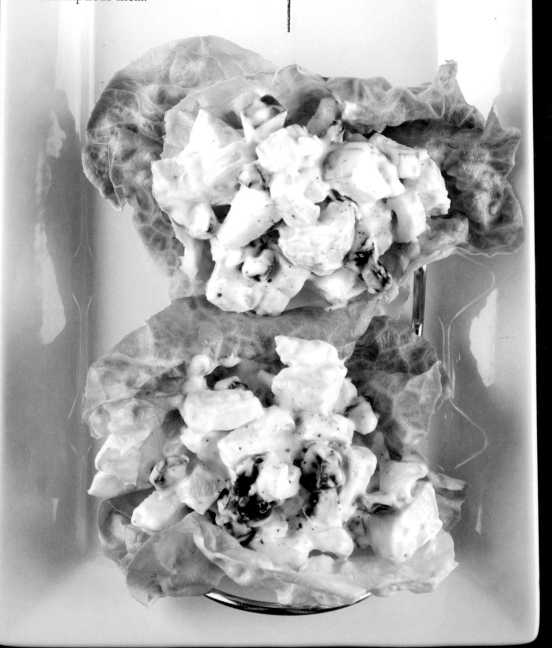

Ingredients

1 head Boston lettuce

1 chicken breast

1 tablespoon olive oil

1 Granny Smith apple

1 celery stalk

¾ cup olive oil mayonnaise

½ teaspoon honey

½ teaspoon Dijon mustard

½ cup dried cranberries

1 teaspoon salt

Tools

paper towels

cutting board

chef's knife

skillet

measuring cups/spoons

tongs

mixing bowl

spoon

Allergen Alert!

Read the label of your mayonnaise carefully to ensure it does not include any allergens you are avoiding.

Dried cranberries are commonly manufactured with nuts, so it's important to check with the manufacturer.

1. Carefully pull off about 8 leaves of lettuce. Rinse well and place on paper towels to dry. Set aside.

2. Cut the chicken breast into 1-inch (2.5-cm) cubes. Add the oil to the skillet and heat over a burner set to medium.

3. Add the chicken and turn the pieces with tongs. Cook until no longer pink inside. When the chicken is done, set aside in the skillet to cool almost completely.

4. Clean your cutting board and knife. Then chop the apple into ½-inch (1.3-cm) cubes and discard the core.

5. Chop the celery into ½-inch (1.3-cm) pieces.

6. Add the apple, celery, mayonnaise, honey, mustard, cranberries, and salt to a mixing bowl. Stir to combine.

7. When the chicken is cooled, add it to the mixing bowl and toss lightly until coated.

8. To assemble the wraps, stack two lettuce leaves on top of each other. Spoon about ½ cup of the chicken salad in the center. Fold the sides in and roll at the same time to envelop the filling.

9. Serve cold, and store leftovers in the refrigerator for up to three days.

CHEF'S TIP

Try using mango, pineapple, or grapes instead of apple. Raisins, dates, or dried apricots can be used instead of dried cranberries.

CHICKEN PARMESAN
STUFFED PEPPERS

What do you get when you cross chicken Parmesan and stuffed peppers? Two mouthwatering entrées rolled into one! Wheat-free bread crumbs top off this recipe to give it a delightful crunch.

Prep Time: 20 minutes

Cook Time: 30 minutes

Serves 4

Ingredients

1 pound (16 oz) chicken breasts

½ teaspoon salt

¼ teaspoon pepper

3 teaspoons olive oil

4 bell peppers

1 cup marinara sauce

4 slices mozzarella cheese

½ cup Parmesan cheese

½ cup wheat-free bread crumbs

Tools

cutting board

chef's knife

measuring cups/spoons

skillet

small mixing bowl

spoon

8 x 8-inch (20 x 20-cm) baking dish

Allergen Alert!

You can still go Italian without all the cheese. Skip the mozzarella and replace the Parmesan with ¼ cup nutritional yeast for a cheesy flavor without the dairy!

1. Preheat oven to 350°F.

2. Cut the chicken breasts in 1-inch (2.5-cm) cubes. Sprinkle salt and pepper on the cubes and set aside.

3. Place 2 teaspoons olive oil in a skillet and place on a burner set to medium heat.

4. Add the chicken and cook until no longer pink inside, about five to six minutes.

5. While the chicken cooks, cut off the tops of the bell peppers and scoop out the seeds and white ribs inside.

6. Pour the marinara sauce in with the chicken and stir until coated.

7. Place 1 slice of mozzarella cheese in the bottom of each pepper.

8. Evenly scoop the chicken into each pepper.

9. In a small bowl, combine the Parmesan cheese, bread crumbs, and 1 teaspoon olive oil and stir.

10. Sprinkle the bread crumb mixture evenly over the top of each pepper.

11. Place the peppers in the baking dish. Bake for about 30 minutes or until the peppers are slightly tender and topping is golden brown.

12. Serve hot.

SWEET POTATO
SHEPHERD'S PIE

Warm and comforting, this dish is sure to satisfy your hunger. As an added bonus, it is also rich in vitamins and protein. Have fun serving up a sweetened, wheat-free spin on this English classic.

Prep Time: 15 minutes

Cook Time: 1 hour

Serves 4

Ingredients

4 medium sweet potatoes

2 quarts water

1 small onion

1 teaspoon olive oil

1 pound (16 oz) lean ground beef or turkey

1 cup beef broth

1 teaspoon coconut aminos

1 tablespoon tomato paste

1 teaspoon garlic powder

4 tablespoons butter

1 teaspoon salt

½ teaspoon ground black pepper

¼ teaspoon paprika

1 cup frozen vegetable mix (carrots, corn, peas)

Tools

vegetable peeler

chef's knife

cutting board

measuring cups/spoons

medium pot

large skillet

spoon

colander

potato masher

8 x 8-inch (20 x 20-cm) baking dish spatula

1. Preheat oven to 325°F.

2. Peel and chop the potatoes. Place them in the pot and fill with water. Place on a burner set to high heat and boil. Reduce heat to medium and cook for 15 minutes or until tender.

3. Peel and chop the onion. Set aside.

4. Place skillet on a burner and set to medium heat. Add oil and onions. Cook for two minutes, stirring gently.

5. Place meat in skillet and break up into small pieces with a spoon. Cook until no longer pink, about eight minutes.

6. Add the broth, aminos, tomato paste, and garlic powder to the skillet. Stir to combine. Reduce heat to low and allow to simmer gently.

7. Drain the potatoes, return to pot, and mash. Add butter, salt, pepper, and paprika. Mash until smooth.

8. Add frozen vegetables to the skillet. Stir to combine.

9. Pour the meat mixture into the baking dish. Spread potatoes on top with a spatula.

10. Bake for 40 minutes, or until the top of the sweet potatoes is slightly browned.

11. Allow to cool for five minutes before serving hot in bowls.

CHEF'S TIP

Not sweet on sweet potatoes? You can use regular white potatoes in this recipe instead.

CREAMY
MAC AND CHEESE

Does your mouth water at the thought of ooey, gooey cheese? If so, then this recipe is for you! Satisfy your comfort food craving with a bowl of this delicious pasta dish that is rich in calcium.

Prep Time: 15 minutes

Cook Time: 15 minutes

Serves 4

Ingredients

8 ounces sharp cheddar cheese

2 quarts water

2 teaspoons salt

2 cups dry wheat-free pasta, such as rice pasta

2 tablespoons butter

2 tablespoons rice flour

2 cups milk

¼ teaspoon ground mustard

¼ teaspoon paprika

Tools

box grater

cutting board

large pot

measuring cups/spoons

medium saucepan

whisk

colander

spoon

Allergen Alert!

Cheese, butter, and milk a no-go? You can still achieve cheesy greatness by using your favorite dairy-free cheese, butter, and milk replacements.

1. Grate the cheese with a large-holed grater placed on top of a cutting board. Set aside.

2. In the large pot, add the water and salt. Place on a burner set on high heat until the water begins to boil.

3. Add the wheat-free pasta. Reduce the heat to medium-high. Cook according to package directions until just tender.

4. Make cheese sauce while the pasta cooks. In the saucepan, melt butter over medium heat.

5. Add the rice flour and whisk until absorbed. The mixture should look like wet sand.

6. Slowly pour the milk in while whisking to avoid lumps. Bring the mixture to a gentle simmer. Keep whisking until it begins to thicken, about five minutes.

7. Stir in the cheese, ground mustard, and paprika until melted. If the sauce is too thick, add a little milk.

8. When the pasta is done, drain it in a colander and place back into the pot.

9. Pour the cheese sauce over the pasta and stir until coated with the sauce.

10. Serve hot in bowls.

CHEF'S TIP

Add your favorite vegetables or toppings such as broccoli, carrots, asparagus, tomatoes, bacon, chicken, or beef!

TACO LETTUCE CUPS

Some taco shells contain wheat, but that doesn't mean you have to take tacos off the menu! Using Boston lettuce leaves as the shells, you can whip up some tasty tacos in no time! Top these leafy "shells" with your favorite veggies and taco toppings!

Prep Time: 20 minutes

Cook Time: 15 minutes

Serves 4

114

Ingredients

1 pound (16 oz) lean ground beef or turkey

1 tablespoon chili powder

1 teaspoon ground cumin

½ teaspoon ground oregano

½ teaspoon paprika

½ teaspoon black pepper

¼ teaspoon onion powder

¼ teaspoon garlic powder

1 teaspoon salt

1 head Boston lettuce

Taco Fixings

corn

beans

tomatoes

avocados

onion

your favorite cheese

salsa

Tools

skillet

spoon

measuring spoons

clean kitchen towel

cutting board

chef's knife

serving bowls

1. In a skillet, brown the ground beef or turkey over medium heat, breaking up the meat into small pieces with a spoon.

2. Add the chili powder, cumin, oregano, paprika, black pepper, onion powder, garlic powder, and salt. Stir to combine and reduce heat to low.

3. Carefully remove the outer leaves from the head of lettuce and dispose of them. Pull off 12 leaves and wash them gently under cool running water. Pat them dry with the clean kitchen towel and set aside.

4. Prepare your taco fixings by chopping tomatoes into small pieces, dicing the avocado, cutting the onion, and grating the cheese. Place in bowls for serving.

5. Transfer the meat to a serving bowl and scoop about 2 tablespoons of meat into each lettuce cup. Then add fixings to your liking.

6. Wrap up tightly and enjoy.

CHEF'S TIP

Vegetarians, don't fret! You can skip the meat and use one can of drained black beans instead. You can also use 2 cups of chopped eggplant or butternut squash in step 1.

Allergens Eradicated!

No major food allergens found here!

DESSERTS

DAIRY-FREE **EGG-FREE** **NUT-FREE** **SOY-FREE** **WHEAT-FREE**

BANANA
ICE CREAM

p.124

LEMON
CUPCAKES
p.122

NO-NUT
BRITTLE
p.130

STRAWBERRY ICE CREAM

WHEAT-FREE

SOY-FREE

EGG-FREE

DAIRY-FREE

Did you know you can combine just four ingredients to make ice cream? Eggs make ice cream rich, but you won't miss them in this sweet summer dessert that can be made or eaten any time of the year.

Prep Time: 10 minutes

Serves 4

118

Ingredients

1 pound (16 oz) frozen strawberries

1 tablespoon sugar

1 teaspoon almond extract

2 tablespoons coconut cream

Tools

food processor

measuring spoons

spatula

bowls, for serving

Allergen Alert!

If you are allergic to nuts, use vanilla extract in place of almond extract.

Coconut is classified as a fruit. But if you have a tree nut allergy, please talk to your doctor before eating it.

1. Place the frozen strawberries, sugar, and almond extract in a food processor and pulse it 10 times.

2. Turn the food processor on high until the mix looks as fluffy as soft-serve ice cream.

3. Scrape down the sides of the bowl with the spatula and pour in the coconut cream.

4. Pulse another 5 times and transfer to bowls for serving immediately.

5. Put leftovers in an airtight container in the freezer right away.

CHEF'S TIP

Substitute blueberries, raspberries, or blackberries for the strawberries if you prefer.

COCONUT VANILLA
PUDDING

Are you craving thick, delicious pudding but need to avoid eggs? Creamy and sweet, this delectable pudding can be made for your entire family or scooped into individual servings to take to school in your lunchbox.

Prep Time: 10 minutes

Cook Time: 4 hours (4 hours inactive)

Serves 4

120

Ingredients

2 cups coconut milk

½ cup sugar

3 tablespoons arrowroot powder

2 teaspoons vanilla extract

pinch of kosher salt

Tools

medium saucepan

measuring cups/spoons

whisk

mixing bowl

large bowl, for serving

Allergen Alert!

Coconut is classified as a fruit. But if
you have a tree nut allergy, please talk
to your doctor before eating it.

1. Place the coconut milk in a saucepan over medium heat. Bring to a simmer.

2. While the coconut milk heats, combine the remaining ingredients in a mixing bowl.

3. When the milk begins to simmer, slowly pour the sugar mixture into the saucepan, whisking while pouring to dissolve.

4. Continue to stir gently until the mixture begins to thicken.

5. Pour pudding into a serving bowl. Chill for at least four hours before serving.

6. Store leftovers in an airtight container in the refrigerator for up to one week.

CHEF'S TIP

Top the pudding with your favorite fruits
or cookie crumbles for extra flavor!

LEMON **CUPCAKES**

Skipping cake because of the eggs? Think again! You can enjoy the cake you've been dreaming of, just without the eggs. Slightly sweet and tart to your tongue, these cupcakes are sure to please.

Prep Time: 15 minutes

Cook Time: 25 minutes

Serves 12

122

Ingredients

cooking spray

2 cups all-purpose flour

1 cup sugar

pinch of kosher salt

2 teaspoons baking powder

½ cup oil, such as grapeseed oil

1 cup milk (any kind)

2 lemons

Glaze

2 lemons

½ cup confectioner's sugar

Tools

standard muffin pan

2 mixing bowls

measuring cups/spoons

wooden spoon

box grater

cutting board

chef's knife

toothpick

small mixing bowl

fork

Allergen Alert!

Are you trying to avoid wheat? Wheat-free flour blend can replace the all-purpose flour in this recipe.

1. Preheat oven to 350°F. Lightly spray a muffin pan with cooking spray. Set aside.

2. Combine the flour, sugar, baking powder, salt, and baking powder in a large mixing bowl. Set aside.

3. Combine the oil and milk in a second bowl. Set aside.

4. Rinse the lemons. Carefully zest the outer yellow part of the rind using the side of the box grater with the small round holes. Add the zest to the oil and milk mixture.

5. Cut 2 lemons in half and squeeze the juice into the oil and milk mixture. Be careful to avoid seeds. Stir to combine.

6. Add the wet ingredients to the dry ingredients and mix well.

7. Fill each muffin cup two-thirds full. Bake for 20 to 25 minutes or until a toothpick inserted into the center comes out clean.

8. Make the glaze while the cupcakes bake. Cut 2 lemons in half and squeeze the juice into a mixing bowl.

9. Add the confectioner's sugar and mix with a fork until dissolved.

10. Remove the cupcakes from the oven and allow to cool completely. After the cupcakes have cooled, remove them from the pan and drizzle the glaze evenly over the tops.

11. Store leftovers in an airtight container for up to one week.

BANANA ICE CREAM

Ice cream is a dessert loaded with dairy. But you can still go cold and creamy with a simple banana creation. You only need two ingredients to make this imitation ice cream on a hot summer day!

Prep Time: 2 hours and 10 minutes
(2 hours inactive)

Serves 4

124

Ingredients

4 very ripe bananas

½ teaspoon vanilla extract

Tools

cutting board

butter knife

freezer-safe zip-top bag

food processor or blender

Allergens Eradicated!

No major food allergens found here!

1. Peel the bananas and slice into 1-inch (2.5-cm) thick rounds on a cutting board.

2. Put the banana rounds into a zip top bag and place in a freezer for at least two hours.

3. Add the frozen bananas and vanilla extract to a food processor or blender. Use the pulse button to chop the bananas into chunks.

4. Set the food processor or blender on high speed. Closely watch the bananas blend until they have a consistency like soft-serve ice cream. It can take several minutes.

5. Serve immediately, or freeze in an airtight, freezer-safe container and keep for up to one week.

CHEF'S TIP

Add mix-ins such as strawberries, raspberries, mangoes, or allergen-free chocolate to your ice cream!

HOT CHOCOLATE
WITH WHIPPED CREAM

No dairy, no problem. You can still warm up on a cold winter's evening with a hot mug of this chocolatey delight!

Prep Time: 8 hours 10 minutes
(8 hours inactive)

Cook Time: 5 minutes

Serves 4

Ingredients

Coconut Whipped Cream

1 8-ounce can coconut cream

½ cup confectioner's sugar

½ teaspoon vanilla extract

Hot Chocolate

1 quart rice milk or
    unsweetened almond milk

½ cup semisweet cocoa powder

½ cup pure honey

2 teaspoons vanilla extract

Tools

can opener

medium mixing bowl

electric hand mixer with
    whisk attachment

measuring cups/spoons

large saucepan

spoon

Allergen Alert!

If you have a tree nut allergy, make sure
    your chocolate is certified nut-free.

1. Place the can of coconut cream in the refrigerator overnight or for at least eight hours before whipping.

2. Add the cream to a medium-sized mixing bowl.

3. Using the electric hand mixer on high, whip the coconut cream until light and fluffy.

4. Add the confectioner's sugar and vanilla extract. Whip on high for another 30 seconds until combined. Place finished cream in refrigerator.

5. Make the hot chocolate while the whipped cream chills. Combine all the hot chocolate ingredients in a large saucepan and stir well.

6. Place over a burner on medium heat. Slowly heat the liquid to avoid burning the chocolate. When it just begins to bubble, it's ready.

7. Pour hot chocolate into mugs and top with a dollop of coconut whipped cream.

8. Store leftover coconut cream in an airtight container in refrigerator for up to one week.

BERRY NUTRITIOUS **SMOOTHIE**

Who says you need milk to make a super thick shake? With a blender and some fruity flavors, you can turn your kitchen into a smoothie stand to make this sweet treat that's easy to make and take with you!

Prep Time: 5 minutes

Makes 1 smoothie

128

Ingredients

1 cup frozen mixed berries

1 banana

¾ cup rice milk

2 tablespoons honey

½ teaspoon vanilla extract

Tools

measuring cups/spoons

blender

Allergens Eradicated!

No major food allergens found here!

1. Combine the frozen berries, banana, rice milk, honey, and vanilla extract in the pitcher of a blender.

2. Pulse 5–6 times to break up the chunks, and then turn to high until smooth.

3. Serve in a glass and enjoy immediately.

CHEF'S TIP

For a super thick smoothie, add a handful of ice cubes to the blender.

BRITTLE

What do you get when you take the peanuts out of peanut brittle? No-nut brittle! Pumpkin seeds add to the crunch in this caramel-flavored candy.

Prep Time: 10 minutes

Cook Time: 2 ½ hours
(2 hours inactive)

Serves 10–12

Ingredients

½ cup white sugar

½ cup brown sugar

4 ounces corn syrup

1 cup pumpkin seeds

1 teaspoon butter

½ teaspoon vanilla extract

½ teaspoon maple extract

1 teaspoon baking soda

Tools

8 x 8-inch (20 x 20-cm)
    baking dish

parchment paper

measuring cups/spoons

large microwave-safe mixing bowl

spatula

Allergen Alert!

Butter can be replaced with a
dairy-free butter in this recipe for
those who are avoiding dairy.

1. Line a baking dish with parchment paper and set aside.

2. In a mixing bowl, combine the white sugar, brown sugar, and corn syrup. Microwave on high for three minutes.

3. Carefully remove from microwave and add the pumpkin seeds. Stir to combine.

4. Return bowl to microwave and cook on high for an additional three minutes.

5. Remove bowl from the microwave. Add the butter, vanilla extract, and maple extract. Stir carefully.

6. Microwave on high for one minute.

7. Remove from microwave and add the baking soda. Stir to combine.

8. Pour into prepared baking dish, and allow to sit for at least two hours to cool.

9. When cooled, break into pieces for serving.

10. Store leftovers in an airtight container at room temperature for up to one week.

CHEF'S TIP

Don't mess with the crunch! Replace
pumpkin seeds with other seeds such
as sesame or sunflower seeds.

CHOCOLATE SUNFLOWER CUPS

Give the traditional peanut butter cup a nut-free makeover! Delight your taste buds by combining smooth milk chocolate and creamy sunflower butter into one delectable, bite-sized dessert.

Prep Time: 1 hour 10 minutes (1 hour inactive)

Makes 1 dozen cups

Ingredients

cooking spray

½ cup sunflower butter

¼ cup confectioner's sugar

¼ teaspoon salt

1 cup semi-sweet chocolate chips

Tools

mini muffin tin

12 mini muffin liners

mixing bowl

measuring cups/spoons

spatula

microwave-safe bowl

Allergen Alert!

Chocolate chips can contain or be manufactured with soy, nuts, and dairy. Make sure to check that the chocolate chips you use are free of allergens.

1. Place 12 mini muffin liners in a mini muffin tin. Spray a small amount of cooking spray in each liner and set aside.

2. In a mixing bowl, combine the sunflower butter, confectioner's sugar, and salt. Mix until thickened. Add more confectioner's sugar if needed.

3. Divide the dough into 12 pieces. Roll each piece between your palms to make 12 small balls. Set aside.

4. In a microwave-safe bowl, melt the chocolate chips by cooking on medium for two minutes. Stir, and then cook on medium an additional minute.

5. To assemble, spread a small amount of chocolate in each liner, followed by a sunflower butter ball. Top with remaining chocolate, until the ball is covered.

6. Place in refrigerator to cool for at least one hour.

7. Store leftovers in refrigerator for up to one week, or in freezer for up to one month.

CHOCOLATE DRIZZLE
RICE TREATS

Ready for dessert? Crispy and sweet, these rice treats can be a delectable finish to a soy-free meal.

Prep Time: 10 minutes

Cook Time: 1 hour (30 minutes inactive)

Makes 24 squares

Ingredients

½ cup honey

½ cup sunflower butter

1 tablespoon butter

4 cups puffed rice cereal

> Chocolate Drizzle

½ cup semi-sweet chocolate chips

1 teaspoon coconut oil

Tools

2 small saucepans

measuring cups/spoons

large mixing bowl

spatula

9 x 13-inch (23 x 33-cm) baking dish

fork

chef's knife

1. Combine honey, sunflower butter, and butter in a small saucepan over medium heat. Allow the butter to melt. Mix well until runny.

2. Add the rice cereal to the mixing bowl. Pour the honey mixture in, stirring with a spatula to coat the cereal well.

3. Using the spatula, press the mixture into a baking dish and allow to cool.

4. While the rice cereal treats cool, make the drizzle. In a saucepan, combine the chocolate chips with the coconut oil over low heat. Stir frequently to avoid burning.

5. When the chips are melted, drizzle the chocolate over the treats with a fork.

6. Allow to cool completely and cut into 24 squares with the chef's knife.

7. Keep leftovers covered at room temperature for up to a week.

Allergen Alert!

Check the labels and contact the manufacturers of your rice cereal and chocolate chips to make sure they are free of allergens you are avoiding.

If you're avoiding dairy, make sure to use a butter substitute instead of regular butter.

Coconut is classified as a fruit. But if you have a tree nut allergy, please talk to your doctor before eating it.

SOY-FREE NUT-FREE EGG-FREE

PEACH AND BLUEBERRY
CRUMBLE

Let's get ready to crumble! Dual fruity flavors will tantalize your taste buds with this soy-free dessert. The crumbly topping provides a crunch but also melts in your mouth.

Prep Time: 15 minutes

Cook Time: 45 minutes

Serves 8

136

Ingredients

4 ripe peaches, fresh or frozen

2 cups blueberries, fresh or frozen

2 tablespoons lemon juice

2 tablespoons arrowroot powder

½ teaspoon ground cinnamon

½ cup rice flour

½ cup packed dark brown sugar

¼ cup oats

¼ cup cold butter

Tools

cutting board

chef's knife

2 mixing bowls

measuring cups/spoons

spatula

8 x 8-inch (20 x 20-cm) baking dish

Allergen Alert!

If you're avoiding dairy, skip the butter and go for a butter substitute.

If you are allergic to wheat, make sure the oats are wheat-free.

1. Preheat oven to 375°F.

2. Remove the pits from the peaches and cut into ¼-inch (0.6-cm) slices. Place in mixing bowl.

3. Add blueberries, lemon juice, arrowroot powder, and cinnamon to the bowl and stir.

4. Pour the fruit into the bottom of a baking dish. Set aside.

5. In a second mixing bowl, combine the rice flour, brown sugar, and oats. Set aside.

6. Cut the butter into tiny pieces and add to the bowl, then stir.

7. Sprinkle the topping over the peaches and blueberries.

8. Bake for about 45 minutes, or until the top is golden brown.

9. Cut into 8 pieces and serve warm.

CHEF'S TIP

If it isn't peach season, don't be afraid of frozen peaches. Frozen fruits and vegetables are picked at the peak of their season and frozen immediately. This keeps the freshness and nutrition packed inside. Just let them thaw, and then drain the liquid before you add them to your dish.

APPLE CAKE

Apple pie is a classic American dessert, but have you ever tried apple cake? Besides being delicious, apples are also high in Vitamin C and fiber. Enjoy making this cake studded with pieces of autumn's favorite fruit!

Prep Time: 20 minutes

Cook Time: 45 minutes

Serves 6

Ingredients

cooking spray

2 cups wheat-free flour blend

1 teaspoon cinnamon

1 teaspoon baking soda

1 teaspoon baking powder

¼ teaspoon salt

1 ½ cups sugar

¾ cup light olive oil

1 teaspoon vanilla extract

3 eggs

3 tart apples

Tools

8 x 8-inch (20 x 20-cm)
  baking dish

2 medium mixing bowls

measuring cups/spoons

electric mixer

vegetable peeler

cutting board

chef's knife

toothpick

Allergen Alert!

If you need to avoid eggs, substitute
  1 ½ cups applesauce in the batter.

1. Preheat oven to 350° F. Spritz the baking dish lightly with cooking spray and set aside.

2. In a mixing bowl, combine the wheat-free flour blend, cinnamon, baking soda, baking powder, and salt.

3. In another mixing bowl, add the sugar, oil, vanilla extract, and eggs.

4. Using an electric mixer set to medium speed, mix the wet ingredients until blended.

5. Pour the wet ingredients into the bowl with dry ingredients. Mix on medium speed until smooth. Set aside.

6. Peel the apples with a vegetable peeler. Chop into small pieces.

7. Transfer half of the batter into the baking dish. Evenly sprinkle apples on top. Pour the remaining batter over them.

8. Place in the oven and bake for about 45 minutes, or until a toothpick comes out clean when inserted.

SUNFLOWER BUTTER
COOKIES

With the help of sunflower butter, you can make a nut-free dessert with a nutty flavor! Crunchy on the outside and soft on the inside, these simple cookies are made with only six ingredients.

Prep Time: 10 minutes

Cook Time: 10 minutes

Makes 1 dozen cookies

Ingredients

2 tablespoons flaxseed meal

¼ cup water

1 cup sunflower butter

¾ cup sugar

¼ cup brown sugar

½ cup allergen-free chocolate chips

Tools

baking sheet

parchment paper

measuring cups/spoons

mixing bowl

spatula

cooling rack

Allergens Eradicated!

No major food allergens found here!

1. Preheat the oven to 350°F. Line a baking sheet with parchment paper.

2. In a mixing bowl, combine the flaxseed meal and water. Stir and allow to sit for five minutes before continuing.

3. Add the sunflower butter, sugar, and brown sugar to the flaxseed mixture. Stir well until it begins to thicken, about one minute.

4. Stir in the chocolate chips.

5. Divide the dough into 12 equally sized pieces. Roll into balls between your palms.

6. Place the dough balls on the baking sheet, evenly spaced. Leave at least 2 inches (5.1 cm) of space between the balls.

7. Use your palm to flatten each dough ball slightly.

8. Place in the oven and bake for about 10 minutes.

9. Remove from oven and allow to cool for five minutes before transferring to a cooling rack.

10. Serve warm or at room temperature and store leftovers in an airtight container for up to three days.

INDEX

Fearless Food is published by Capstone Young Readers, a Capstone Imprint
1710 Roe Crest Drive, North Mankato, Minnesota 56003
www.mycapstone.com

Library of Congress Cataloging-in-Publication Data
Cataloging-in-Publication data is on file with the Library of Congress.
ISBN 978-1-62370-608-1 (paperback)
ISBN 978-1-62370-609-8 (eBook PDF)

Editorial Credits
Anna Butzer, editor; Heidi Thompson and Tracy McCabe, designers;
Morgan Walters, media researcher;
Sarah Schuette, food stylist; Kathy McColley, production specialist

Design Elements
Shutterstock: avian, design element, Katerina Kirilova, design element, Lena Pan,
design element, Marco Govel, design element, mexrix, design element, Sabina Pittak,
design element, STILLFX, design element, swatchandsoda, design element

Photography by Capstone Studio: Karon Dubke

Editor's note:
Capstone cannot ensure that any food is allergen-free. The only way to be sure a
food is safe is to read all labels carefully, every time. Cross-contamination is also
a risk for those with food allergies. Please call food companies to make sure their
manufacturing processes avoid cross-contamination. Also, always be sure to clean
hands, surfaces, and tools before cooking.

Printed and bound in the USA.
010102S17